In the Shadow of Our Ancestors

The Inventions and Genius of the First Peoples

ESCHIA
BOOKS

Wayne Arthurson

The Publisher: Eschia Books Inc.

Library and Archives Canada Cataloguing in Publication

Arthurson, Wayne, 1962–
In the shadow of our ancestors: the inventions and genius of the
First Peoples / Wayne Arthurson.

Includes bibliographical references.

ISBN 978-1-926696-13-3

1. Indians of North America—Intellectual life. I. Title.
E77.A78 2011   970.004'97   C2011-901379-7

Project Director: Kathy van Denderen
Editor: Volker Bodegom
Photo Credits: Every effort has been made to accurately credit the sources
of photographs. Any errors or omissions should be reported directly to
the publisher for correction in future editions. Photographs courtesy of
Library of Congress (p. 10, LC-USZ62-105062; p. 19, LC-USZ62- 3000;
p. 48, LC-USZ62-130207; p. 57, LC-USZ62-111135;
p. 77, LC-USZ62-56418; p. 94, LC-USZ62-127674;
p. 103, LC-DIG-ggbain-00161; p. 113, LC-DIG-pga-02616;
p. 127, LC-DIG-pga-02687; p. 138, LC-USZ62-92635;
p. 160, LC-USZ62-69316; p. 171, LC-USZ62-56416;
p. 187, LC-USZC4-7925; p. 207, LC-USZC4-7214;
p. 216, LC-USZC2-1189; p. 225, LC-USA7-27850;
p. 236, LC-USZ62-20214; p. 238, LC-USZ62-93141), U.S. Geological
Survey (p. 26), Wikipedia Commons (p. 33, from Iowa Office of the State
Archaeologist collection; p. 36, from Public Library of Science, Mauricio
Anton; p. 68, from Oklahoma Historical Society; p. 74, from United
States Mint; p. 92, from United States Department of Agriculture;
p. 211; p. 230, from Library of Congress Map Division, g4050 ct000654).
Cover Image: © Hemera Technologies

We acknowledge the support of the Province of Alberta through Alberta
Foundation for the Arts.

We acknowledge the support of the Canada Council for the Arts which
last year invested $20.1 million in writing and publishing throughout
Canada.

Contents

Author's Note 5

Introduction 8

CHAPTER 1: **Who Were These People?** 18

CHAPTER 2: **A Modern Theory for the Origin of
Native Americans.** 25

CHAPTER 3: **The Clovis Point** 29

CHAPTER 4: **The Overkill Theory** 34

CHAPTER 5: **Before Clovis** 47

CHAPTER 6: **The Kayak** 54

CHAPTER 7: **Code Talkers** 64

CHAPTER 8: **The Potato** 75

CHAPTER 9: **The Great Law of Peace** 93

CHAPTER 10: **Saving Jacques Cartier and
New France** 111

CHAPTER 11: **Rescuing Jamestown** 120

CHAPTER 12: **Tobacco** 137

CHAPTER 13: **Maize** 166

CHAPTER 14: **Government Influences** 193

CHAPTER 15: **Equal Rights** 215

CHAPTER 16: **Sacagawea** 229

CHAPTER 17: **The Truth** 241

Appendix 244

Notes on Sources 260

Dedication

To my family

Author's Note

When I began planning to write this book, I knew it would be an intense and difficult undertaking. There would be many books to read, much research to uncover and a multitude of decisions to make on how to approach the subject and the tone of the writing.

At the same time, I also knew this project was worth all this effort. For too long, the accomplishments of Native Americans—be they from what we now call Canada, the United States, Mexico or Central or South America—have been downplayed. Many times they've been ignored, forgotten or had the facts about them just plain distorted and completely changed. For too long, schools have taught that Natives in the Americas were primitive hunters and gatherers who had no influence on modern society and that they were in need of being civilized by the new European settlers. For too long, we've based our ideas of who Native Americans were and what they did on biased and incorrect histories and on movies that showed them to be impediments to civilization, whereas the opposite was true.

The accomplishments of the Natives of the Americas are diverse and astounding. Their influence has been wide-reaching and extraordinary. When I was working on this book, I already knew many of the stories I wrote about. But I discovered many new ones and was further astounded by the things I discovered. As a man of Cree descent, I felt my heart swell with pride every time I read a new fact about something Native Americans discovered or how they influenced our modern world.

One of the main difficulties of writing a book like this is determining how to approach the subject. Should I just make a shopping list of the accomplishments and influences of Native Americans and then write about each one? Or should I approach the writing differently? Well, I'm more of an organic writer, more able and willing to allow the story to flow out of me naturally and see where it takes me. So I went with my strengths. I did all the research I could, and then I started where I felt the story should begin and allowed the process of how to frame the book come to me naturally. I realize this might not make it easy if someone is looking for a specific topic, but I also know this makes for a better story, a better book to read. I decided that I would follow each topic as far as I could. Each one of these accomplishments and influences would be described like a pebble dropped into a lake; the first impact is small and seemingly insignificant, but the ripples spread out, getting wider and wider until they cover the entire lake.

For example, I wouldn't just write that Native Americans offered tobacco to the world. I would follow the route tobacco took into the rest of the world and write about the many impacts and influences tobacco has had on humankind and the planet Earth.

Because of this approach, I didn't cover as many topics as I initially hoped. But I accomplished my first goal, and that is to show that the Natives of the Americas were already an extremely accomplished, complex and sophisticated people before the arrival of the Europeans, and that their influence on global society—not just in the past but today—has been remarkable.

And their accomplishments and contributions should not be forgotten, ignored or denied. They should be remembered and celebrated by all.

Introduction

Christopher Columbus

I n 1492, as history books have trumpeted with much fanfare, Christopher Columbus "discovered" a New World. Many students in North America, particularly in the United States, were taught that Columbus discovered America.

In truth, Columbus never set foot on the land most of us know as America, the United States of America. Out of the four voyages Columbus made to the New World, he reached the mainland only on two of them. During his third voyage, in 1498, he explored a small part of the mainland of South America. On his fourth, in 1502, he explored parts of Central America, including the coastlines of what are now Honduras, Nicaragua, Costa Rica and Panama.

On his first voyage in 1492, the one that made him a household name, Columbus and his crew first discovered an island in the chain we now call the Bahamas. It was in the early morning hours of October 12 when a sailor on the *Pinta* first sighted land.

When they finally made landfall, Columbus was greeted by the inhabitants, a people known as the Lucayan. They were peaceful and friendly, and they presented Columbus and his men with beads, jewelry and leaves of tobacco. About these people, Columbus wrote:

> *Many of the men I have seen have scars on their bodies, and when I made signs to them to find out how this happened, they indicated that people from*

*other nearby islands come to San Salvador to cap-
ture them; they defend themselves the best they can.
I believe that people from the mainland come here to
take them as slaves. They ought to make good and
skilled servants, for they repeat very quickly whatever we say to them. I think they can very easily be
made Christians, for they seem to have no religion.
If it pleases Our Lord, I will take six of them to Your
Highnesses when I depart, in order that they may
learn our language.*

He also noted that they lacked modern weaponry such as swords or pikes. "I could conquer the whole of them with fifty men, and govern them as I pleased," he wrote in his journal.

About two weeks later, Columbus moved on and landed on the island now known as Cuba. Again, he was greeted peacefully by the people of that island, the Guacanagari. They allowed Columbus to leave behind 39 of his men so they could establish the settlement of La Navidad, then known as the first settlement in the New World.

Columbus returned to Spain, declared his discovery and thus became one of the best-known humans in history, the "discoverer of America." Columbus himself did not believe, however, that he had discovered a new land. Even until his death in 1506, Columbus thought he had only discovered islands off the coast of Asia.

Despite Columbus' misconceptions and the myth that he discovered America, the importance of what he did should not be diminished. His achievements were of major historical significance, ones with repercussions—both good and bad—that would be felt throughout the world.

Christopher Columbus lands on the island of San Salvador on October 12, 1492. Although it has been claimed he "discovered" America, there were millions of people already living there.

Columbus' discovery changed the balance of power in Europe, sparked the Age of Exploration in Europe and opened up lands for European countries to colonize and exploit. His discovery also strongly influenced the culture and the way of life for many peoples and ultimately resulted in the further development of "Western" civilization through the creation of countries such as the United States of America, Canada, Mexico, Brazil and all the others on the American continents.

Even so, there are rumblings about whether Columbus actually was the first outsider to "discover" the New World.

The Chinese

In his 2002 book, *1421: The Year China Discovered the World*, Gavin Menzies states that another group of people made it to the American continents decades before Columbus. Accord-ing to the former British submarine commander, ships from a Chinese fleet commanded by the great explorer Admiral Zheng He arrived earlier. The fleet sailed around Africa's Cape of Good Hope and, using currents and the prevailing winds, crossed the Atlantic. The Chinese mariners first reached the Caribbean islands of Guadeloupe and then moved northwestward to Cuba, the author claims.

According to Menzies' book, the Chinese then split up, with separate fleets heading north and south, up the eastern coast of North America, south to Brazil and around Cape Horn and northward along the west coast of South and North America. In many places, it is claimed, they made contact with the inhabit-ants of the land and established settlements, the occupants of which were integrated into many of the Native tribes in North and South America.

Even though historians largely refute Menzies' claims regarding the extent of Chinese exploration, Zheng He and other Chinese admirals were truly great explorers. Zheng He made seven known voyages, traversing over 30,000 miles of ocean from China to Southeast Asia, India and Africa. His great treasure fleets were massive, with ships to carry horses and other animals, water, troops and food. The ships themselves were also on a grand scale. The largest had nine masts, was over 400 feet long and could carry over 1250 tons of cargo. In comparison, Columbus' largest ship, the *Santa Maria*, was only 76 feet long.

Despite the claims made by Menzies, there is no defini-tive evidence to prove the Chinese arrived in the New World before Columbus. But regardless whether ships from Zheng He's fleet did make it to the Americas or not, there is actual proof of earlier visitors to the New World.

The Norsemen

Born in 970 AD, Norse explorer Leif Ericson was an outlaw and explorer. He was the son of Erik Thorvaldsson, aka Erik the Red, who was also an explorer and an outlaw. By the time Ericson was born, his father had established two colonies in Greenland, marking the western extreme of the Norse expansion to date. According to the inhabitants of Greenland who traded with the Norsemen, there were additional lands even farther west.

So, in the year 1002, Leif Ericson and 35 men headed west.

The first land Ericson found was rocky, and he considered it not really suitable for a settlement. Many historians believe this was Baffin Island. Ericson then headed south and made two landfalls, one in northern Labrador and another at the northeastern tip of a land he called Vinland (now Newfoundland).

It was in Vinland where he founded a small settlement and overwintered before returning to Greenland. The winter in Vinland was bitter and harsh, but these were Norsemen, Vikings from the Scandinavian kingdoms of Norway, Sweden and Denmark. By the time Ericson was visiting North America, the Vikings were in the middle of their golden age, ruling throughout Europe, even establishing major trade and administrative routes from Russia to the Byzantine Empire near the Black and Caspian seas. Severely cold winters were nothing to these people.

Ericson returned the next year to Vinland, but neither he nor any Norse explorer after him managed to establish a permanent settlement in this new land. According to some sources, one of the reasons a permanent settlement was never established by the Norse in North America was that the Natives of Vinland were not receptive to the newcomers living there. Too many Norsemen were killed by Native attacks, so the settlement of Vinland was abandoned and mostly forgotten.

For many centuries, the story of Erik the Red and his son Leif Ericson was considered a legend, a story told in two Icelandic sagas, the *Saga of Erik the Red* and the *Saga of the Greenlanders*. Many historians had no doubts that Leif Ericson and his father existed, because the existence of the Greenland settlements had been proven. But because there was no archeological proof, no direct physical evidence to show that Leif Ericson had made it to the North American shore and established a temporary settlement, the idea that someone had arrived before Columbus was considered preposterous.

But unlike the story about the Chinese coming to North America, proof of Norse habitation was actually discovered. In 1960, Helge Ingstad and his wife, Anne Stine, discovered the remnants of a Norse village at L'Anse aux Meadows on the northern tip of Newfoundland. The village was dated at about 1000 years old, matching the dates noted in the Icelandic sagas. The style of the eight buildings matched the buildings the Norse used in Greenland and Iceland at that time. The discovery proved that Leif Ericson—and not Christopher Columbus—was the earliest known "Discoverer of the New World."

However, because Columbus' discovery centuries after Ericson's resulted in permanent European settlement in the New World, Columbus gets greater recognition.

Notice that the various stories about the "discovery of the New World" have similarities that have usually not been considered significant enough to warrant much additional notice. All these "discovery" stories seem to play down that people were already living in these lands.

On the islands of the Caribbean and the coasts of Central and South America, Christopher Columbus encountered Native populations. On the northern tip of Newfoundland, Leif Ericson encountered Natives. Moreover, near the Norse village at L'Anse aux Meadow, archeologists explored the remnants of a Native village that had been inhabited for 6000 years prior to Ericson's arrival.

Even in the story about the Chinese discovery, Native peoples meet with the ships of Zheng He's fleet. According to Gavin Menzies' book, the Natives welcomed the Chinese sailors and made them part of their communities.

In history books around the world, people read and are taught that almost every single European explorer or settler who arrived in the "New World" in the several centuries after Columbus came to the region met Native peoples who had been living on these lands for thousands of years.

And contrary to popular belief for many centuries—even as recently as a decade ago—these people were not primitive savages with no civilization, no organized society, no agriculture and no tools save for the basics required for hunting and gathering. The Native Americans were not "among the most culturally backward people in the world," nor were they "man in the raw state of nature," as inferred by Allan R. Holmberg in his 1950 book, *Nomads of the Long Bow: The Siriono of Eastern Bolivia,* one of the most influential and incorrect texts affecting the image of Natives in the Americas as a whole.

The people who lived on the continents of America were not the people who "created no lasting monuments or institutions" or were "[i]mprisoned in changeless wilderness," as Charles C. Mann (in his 2005 book *1491: New Revelations of the Americas Before Columbus*) summarized the assertions of two-time Pulitzer Prize winner Samuel Eliot Morison in his two-volume *The European Discovery of America*, published in 1971 and 1974.

Pre-Columbian America was not the way many North American high school history textbooks claimed as recently as the early 1990s. For example, it was described as "empty of mankind and its works" in previous editions of Alan Brinkley's *American History: A Survey*. (Author's note: These misconceptions were cleared in the 2009 release of *American History: A Survey*. The first chapter of this popular textbook notes that "there was as much variety among the civilizations of the Americas as among the civilizations of Europe, Asia and Africa." However, only about five pages of the first chapter is devoted to these civilizations. The remaining 577 pages focus mostly on American history as it relates to Europeans and their descendents.)

The truth of the matter is that the people of this "New World" had been living on this landscape for a long period of time, estimated at anywhere from 13,000 to 30,000 years, depending on which archeologist you ask.

According to a number of new archeological finds, because large parts of North and South America were not covered by ice during the last great ice age of about 11,000 years ago, it's quite reasonable to expect that a substantial and thriving population of humans lived on this land. At the same time, though, much of Europe was covered in ice sheets hundreds of feet thick and hundreds of miles wide. As a result, much of the "Old World" of Europe was obviously devoid of people during the period.

And even more archeological evidence is showing that the population of the Americas at the time of Columbus' discovery was larger than the population of Europe at the time. Furthermore, Europeans who arrived after Columbus described the New World not as an empty wilderness but as a place densely filled with people. Even Bartolomé de las Casas, one of the first Catholic bishops in the New World, noted that the mainland of Mexico was "all filled as though the land were a beehive of people," and that it appeared that "God did set down upon these lands the entire multitude, or greatest part, of the entire human lineage."

Contrary to popular belief and myth, most of these people were not limited to forming simple hunting and gathering societies. Instead, most lived in large, well-established communities. They lived in tribes, clans, nations, kingdoms and cultures that thrived for thousands of years. A good number of these societies had been in existence longer than any other established society in the world, be they western or eastern.

Although a large portion of the people of the so-called New World were hunters and gatherers, they were also farmers, builders, architects, scientists, mathematicians, astronomers, engineers, merchants, traders, linguists, priests, philosophers, warriors, artisans, politicians, warmongers and kings. And much more.

They were as diverse, as advanced and as cultured as any other group of people living in other parts of the world at any time in history.

And they left us a great legacy.

Greater than what we have been led to believe.

Chapter One

Who Were These People?

Early Theories

Before we start discussing the impact these original Americans made on the world, we have to discuss who these people were and how they arrived on these continents.

Questions regarding the origins of the people of the Americas caused much consternation among the Europeans when they discovered there was another part of the world they didn't know about.

At first, Columbus (and some of the explorers who followed soon after him) simply believed that they had discovered islands off the coast of China, Japan or India. Ergo, these people were simply Asians. According to legend, Columbus thought these people were from the "Indies" (which was the European name for India and China at the time), so that's why they were originally called "Indians." It's a nice story to explain the mistake, but it never has been proven true.

The man that the Americas were named after, Amerigo Vespucci, is shown landing on the shore. Vespucci was mistakenly touted as the first European to arrive in the Americas.

The idea that these people were Asians and that these lands were new (to the Europeans) islands off the coast of Asia, and that the kingdoms of Cathay (China) and Nippon (Japan) were just around the corner or over the horizon, prevailed for quite some time. Even to his death, Columbus believed he had discovered a new route to Asia. And one day, he thought, some other explorer would actually meet with the Emperor of Cathay, and new trade routes would be established.

Columbus was, obviously, incorrect. These new lands were not Asia. However, his contention about who these people were was much closer to the truth.

Even before Columbus died, others were saying that these were not gateway islands to Asia but actually a whole new continent and its islands. Amerigo Vespucci, originally an Italian, was hired by the Portuguese to travel to these new lands. Some Portuguese explorers had followed the Spanish to these new lands and discovered what are now parts of South America. King Manuel I of Portugal wanted to know if these lands were also islands or were part of a larger continent connected to the lands the Spanish discovered.

Although some of Vespucci's claims and letters have been disputed by scholars, he did inspire at least one idea that took hold. Because of the claims attributed to Vespucci—many of which are now reputed to have been made by others and not by Vespucci himself—a large number of Europeans initially thought that Vespucci, and not Christopher Columbus, was the first one to discover these new lands.

Martin Waldseemüller was a German-born cartographer who in 1507 produced *Universallis Cosmicgrapha*, one of the first maps of the world to show these new lands as a brand-new continent. And based on the idea that Amerigo Vespucci was the discoverer of these lands, Waldseemüller named them "America."

It should be noted that Waldseemüller was limited to the information he had at the time, so his maps weren't entirely accurate. In later editions of his map, he corrected his naming mistake by removing the word "America." He instead used the term *Terra Incognita*, Latin for "Unknown Land." But many copies of his original map remained, and, as more cartographers mapped the world, the name "America" was continually used until it stuck.

Waldseemüller's map also only showed the new continent as a long strip, and not the entire continent we know today. This distortion just reflected what had been discovered and noted by the explorers of the time. But the map did serve an important purpose: it showed that these new lands were not part of Asia. And as more and more people headed out to explore these new lands, they slowly started to realize that they were visiting a brand-new continent.

This realization caused even more consternation about the origins of the people (and the new animals) inhabiting these lands.

But What Does the Bible Say?

According to the Bible, all the people of the Earth were descendents of Adam and Eve. It said that all those descendants, save for the family of Noah, had perished in the Great Flood. All the animals were also destroyed, except for the ones that marched two by two into the ark. And given that scholars of the Bible had determined that Noah's Ark had landed on Mount Ararat, in eastern Turkey, how did these people (and the animals) get to the new continent?

Christian scholars could explain the existence of other non-Christian peoples, such as the Africans, Indians, Chinese and other Asians. These lands were connected to Turkey by land or were separated only by small seas, such as the Mediterranean or the Arabian, and the people could have, in time, easily traveled there from Mount Ararat.

But the new continent was not connected to the already mapped ones. And the Europeans had only just crossed the Atlantic to get there. It wasn't an easy feat by any means. No one, not even the Chinese (except perhaps Zheng He, but they didn't know about him anyway), had yet made it across the Pacific. So how did these people get to the new continents after the Great Flood mentioned in the Bible? If they had arrived there before the deluge, they couldn't have survived the flood because, according to the Bible, God had destroyed all of mankind in that flood, except Noah and his family.

Some grave and incomprehensible questions were asked. Was the Bible wrong about the story of Noah? If it was, did that throw into question everything else in the Bible? And if that *was* the case, was the established book that formed the entire basis of the Christian religion, a book claimed by priests, bishops, popes and monarchs to be the Word of God, no longer to be believed?

Of course, given that Christianity was integral to the fabric of European society, the view that the Bible may be incorrect was unacceptable. Indeed, those questions could barely be asked. Nearly a century after Columbus was greeted by these "new" people, an explanation was given. José de Acosta, a Jesuit scholar who spent 25 years living in the New World, concluded that, in some undiscovered part of the world, Asia and America were connected:

> *If this is true, as indeed it appears to me to be,... we would have to say that they crossed not by sailing on the sea but by walking on land. And they followed this way quite unthinkingly, changing places and lands little by little, with some of them settling in the lands already discovered and others seeking new ones...*

De Acosta's conclusion avoided challenging the correctness of the Bible, because it surmised that these people must have somehow walked from Asia to the Americas at some time after the Great Flood. It's quite interesting to note that de Acosta was much closer to the truth than he realized.

Still, before we go into more accepted origin theories, de Acosta's explanation didn't quell the questions. If these people walked to the Americas, then from which people were they descended? Were they ancient Greeks, Egyptians or Assyrians? Were they Chinese, Basques, Romans, Africans or Hindus? Were they a mythical lost band of Welsh or were they survivors from the destruction of Atlantis? All of these ideas and more were put forward. But the most accepted answer also came from the Bible. These people were the Lost Tribes of Israel.

As described in the second Book of Kings in the Old Testament, the Hebrew tribes fractured into two groups, the north and the south. The capital of the north was Jerusalem, and the capital of the south was Samaria. The north was ruled by the House of David, and its members were more orthodox; the south was ruled by King Omri and his wife Jezebel, and their people weren't. The people of the south had temples to multiple gods, which to the orthodox north went against the Word of God.

Because of this fracture and constant infighting, the land of Israel was vulnerable to attack and was quickly taken over by the Assyrians.

The squabbling 10 tribes were ejected from Israel by the Assyrians. The Bible states that, to repent their sins, the tribe members resolved to go to distant lands never inhabited by humanity. Therefore, many scholars agreed that these original Americans were clearly descendants of the Lost Tribes of Israel.

The originator of the idea that the first Americans came from Asia didn't agree with the Lost Tribes theory, however. The Americans were not circumcised, José de Acosta pointed out. And being a Jesuit priest at the time of the Inquisition, he was not a big fan of the Jews. He believed that Jews were "cowardly and weak." But the Natives of this new land were not like that at all, de Acosta noted. Despite these counterarguments, the Lost Tribes of Israel origin theory prevailed for many centuries and was still popular even into the early 1900s.

For many people, though, where these people had come from was not that important. Even if they were lost Israelis, or even survivors from Atlantis, they were still savage, primitive people, it was said—even the ones who built cities that were bigger than most in Europe. They were no different than the mountains, the rivers and the lakes and everything else on these new continents: they were something to be overcome and exploit4174741ed, egardless of the consequences. And so they were.

Chapter Two

A Modern Theory for the Origin of Native Americans

The questions of who the first inhabitants of the Americas were and how they got there are still very much debated today. The most accepted theory, at least for now, is that the original people of the Americas came from Asia between 10,000 and 13,000 years ago.

These original people arrived in North America via the Bering Strait land bridge, known as Beringia. Because of a massive ice age known as the Late Wisconsin Glacial Period, about 25,000 to 30,000 years ago, sea levels throughout the world dropped dramatically. As a result, large tracts of seabed became exposed for long periods of time. Beringia, one such tract, was a massive land area more than 600 miles wide. Mostly a grassland steppe, Beringia was home to various tribes of people and animals for thousands of years.

The Beringia migration theory states that although many people lived on this landmass for thousands of years, access to the more southern parts of the North American continent and farther along to Central and South America was limited.

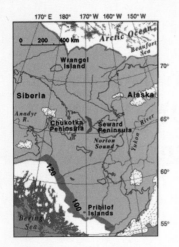 

Left: *Beringia, a large land mass, nearly 1000 miles wide created during the late Wisconsin Glaciations. This grassland steppe was home to many peoples for thousands of years.* **Right:** *A map of western Alaska and eastern Siberia, showing the present-day shorelines.*

Although Beringia itself wasn't covered in ice, a large part of what is now Canada was. Two vast glacier sheets, the Laurentide and the Cordilleran, met near what is now the Alberta–British Columbia border. And these massive glaciers, many of them hundreds of yards high, were impossible to cross, it is believed. Some anthropologists theorized that a small number of people did manage to get through via the corridor of the Rocky Mountains, which were not completely covered in ice. But the proposed number of humans who may have made this journey was too small to be responsible for the population found living in the Americas thousands of years later.

Only when the Earth began to warm and the Laurentide and Cordilleran sheets retreated did a completely ice-free corridor open. It was then that the people of Beringia could move

into what is now southern Alberta and migrate farther into
North America.

Imagine the world these people must have found awaiting
them. It was a true wilderness, unlike what the Europeans
thought of the New World when they first "discovered" it. There
were great rivers and lakes filled with fish. Seemingly endless
plains and massive forests teeming with wildlife. Many of the
animals they encountered—such as bison, deer, antelope, elk and
moose—are still seen today, but in much reduced numbers. There
were also huge creatures that are now extinct: mammoths, mastodons, great armored rhinos, three types of horses, two kinds of
camels, giant beavers as large as couches, turtles as big as cars,
sloths that could stretch up to branches 20 feet above the ground,
plus many others. There were also predators—such as lions similar to those in Africa, saber-toothed cats and dire wolves—which
presented some problems for the newly arriving humans but also
represented additional kinds of potential prey.

Many of the species of wildlife that could be hunted
had never seen humans before. They didn't consider people to be
predators, so when the humans came close, it has been suggested,
they usually didn't flee. So, the theory goes, for the humans in
this New World, much of this game was relatively easy to hunt.

The climate was also warmer, especially as the new
inhabitants moved farther south. Thus, life was much easier
than during the ice age of their great-great-grandparents. And
although the land bridge had by now receded underwater and cut
off further migration from Asia, there were enough humans
already in North America to populate the continent in a relatively
short period of time.

According to Paul Martin, a professor from the University of Arizona, a group of 100 people in this rich environment could double their population every 20 years. In about 400 years, that original group could result in a population of one million. And one million Paleo-Indians could easily have distributed themselves across North and South America, from Alaska to Tierra del Fuego, in 1000 years.

The foregoing is the most popular theory on how the Americas became populated millennia before Columbus. According to this theory, these people spread and changed the entire landscape of the Americas. Every indigenous culture in North, Central and South America is believed to be descended from these people.

Because of where their first artifacts were found, anthropologists named them the "Clovis" people.

Chapter Three

The Clovis Point

I n 1929, a Native American ironically named Ridgely Whiteman was a 19-year-old high school graduate living in Clovis, New Mexico. His mother was a Native woman from Ohio who had a large collection of arrowheads from Ohio. That collection sparked the young man's interest in American Indian lore. As a Boy Scout, he spent much time outdoors, camping and surveying the area around Clovis.

Like many people in Clovis, Whiteman collected Native artifacts from a dry river bend just south of town. He decided, however, to take his collecting one step further. A few years earlier, in 1926, there had been an important archeological find in the town of Folsom, New Mexico, a town about 175 miles to the north. An amateur archeologist had found some bison bones and artifacts indicating that people had arrived in North America several thousand years earlier than previously thought.

Aware of this nearby discovery, Whiteman thought his Native artifacts had some scientific value. Therefore, he sent some of his findings, along with a letter, to the Smithsonian in Washington, DC.

Surprisingly, the Smithsonian replied to this unknown Boy Scout. A paleontologist named Charles Gilmore took the train from Washington, DC, to Clovis. Even though Gilmore probably spent several days on the train to get to Clovis, he didn't spend much time at the actual discovery site. He walked around the area with Whiteman for only an hour. Then he declared the site unimportant to the world of paleontology, archeology and anthropology, and grabbed the next train out of town.

Young Whiteman was surprised by Gilmore's reaction, but if he had known more about the state of the science surrounding Paleo-Indians of that time, he wouldn't have been. The establishment in the fields of archeology and anthropology wasn't very open to new ideas regarding the origins of Paleo-Indians.

Since shortly after Columbus' arrival, the Lost Tribes of Israel theory had prevailed. Even around the time Whiteman had sent his artifacts to the Smithsonian, a large segment of the population still believed the Lost Tribes theory.

One must also remember that there was some resistance to certain types of scientific theories at that time. For example, just four years prior to Whiteman's find, in 1925, a high school biology teacher had been convicted of the crime of teaching evolution to his students.

And the existence of any humans living in North America thousands of years before Jesus, or before people had settled in Europe, didn't match the thinking of the period. Many Christian leaders refused to believe any such theories, even those backed up by evidence, because it contradicted their doctrine. Many scientists of the time also refused to believe humans had lived in the Americas for so long, despite the reams of evidence presented to them.

The founder and long-time editor of the *American Journal of Physical Anthropology* was one of these scientists. For the first few decades of the 20th century, Aleš Hrdlička dismissed any and all discoveries of bones and artifacts that showed humans inhabited North America during the Pleistocene period, a section of geological time that began 2.5 million years ago and ended 10,000 years ago.

Hrdlička was so thorough in his dismissal of all finds that many anthropologists realized that to oppose him, even with evidence, could ruin their careers. Therefore, many would-be dissenters kept quiet and followed the status quo.

But Whiteman was not a professional scientist. He had no scientific reputation to uphold or a tenured job to protect. He believed his findings meant something, so he kept pushing, kept sending letters and samples to various scientists throughout the country. Finally, in 1932, he got in contact with Edgar B. Howard, a graduate student from the University of Pennsylvania. Howard examined Whiteman's artifacts in Philadelphia and then traveled to Clovis in 1933.

Howard established an archeological dig at the site where Whiteman had found his artifacts. For four years, Howard and his workers carefully excavated the site, which became known as the Blackwater Locality Number 1.

Subsequently, the area become known as one of the most significant archeological sites in North America and was declared a National Historic Landmark in 1961.

Two important discoveries were made at the Blackwater Locality.

Prior to the Clovis discovery, the Folsom dig a few years earlier had pushed against the dogma that no people could have been living in the Americas more than 9000 years ago. The Clovis discovery pretty much destroyed that idea. In one fell swoop, the established theories of the time, and the prevailing Lost Tribes of Israel doctrine, were crushed under the weight of overwhelming evidence. There was no longer any doubt that people had been living in the Americas during the Pleistocene period. And not only that, they had thrived. Once the Clovis discovery was announced to the world, similar sites were found throughout North America, showing that the Clovis culture, as it came to be called, had been widespread throughout the continent. And when carbon dating was invented in the 1950s, all the Clovis sites were consistently dated between 13,500 and 12,900 years ago. At the time, the Clovis culture was the oldest known Paleo-Indian culture of North America, and this theory of the population of the Americas still has many supporters in the archeological and anthropological communities, despite some recent finds of even older habitation sites.

The key element of the Clovis culture is the spear point that these people developed, commonly known as the Clovis point. About four inches long and cut with a concave end with shallow channels, or flutes, into the head, the Clovis point was a technological marvel for its period. Hunters of the time would set the end of the spear into the flute and then fasten it with thin cord made out of animal hide. If the head of the stone point chipped or broke off, the Clovis point could be slid forward on the shaft and a new point could be chipped.

Samples of Clovis points from the Iowa Office of the State Archaeologist collection. Note the flutes on the bottoms.

No other indigenous culture in the world at the time—or even later—developed this style of fluting on their spearheads. The Clovis point was a uniquely American invention.

The development of this spearhead allowed these people to be excellent hunters. And as noted earlier, the land they inhabited was filled with a plethora of creatures. In all, scientists have discovered that the Clovis people used their technologically advanced spearhead to hunt over 125 species, including bison, sloths, tapirs, horses, lions, wolves and saber-toothed cats, as well as the two largest animals on the continent, mastodons and wooly mammoths.

Some scientists believe that the Clovis people were *too* good as hunters. They go so far as to say that the Clovis people not only caused many animals to become extinct and changed the landscape of the continent, but they also sealed the fate of their descendants when they first met the Europeans.

Chapter Four

The Overkill Theory

While scientists were studying the artifacts left by the Clovis people, they made a few discoveries. For example, they realized that despite the Clovis people being the ancestors of all indigenous people of the Americas, the lifespan of Clovis culture was relatively short, only about 500 years.

They also discovered that Clovis culture had disappeared from the landscape at the same time as many of the animals they hunted. One theory that has gained a lot of traction is that the Clovis people were responsible for the deaths of many of these animals, eliminating a large part of their own food source. Thus, the Clovis were responsible for their own demise, it was proposed.

This theory is known as the Pleistocene Overkill Hypothesis. It was first put forward in the 1960s by University of Arizona zoology professor Paul Martin. The overkill theory states that the Clovis people were a highly mobile group, armed with one of the most technologically advanced weapons of the time, the Clovis point. They were also proficient hunters, adept at taking down even the largest animals on the continent. And North America at the time was filled with many immense animals, which are called megafauna. They included mammoths, mastodons, an extinct species of bison, armored rhinos, saber-toothed cats, giant sloths, giant turtles and others.

A large number of smaller animals that lived in North America during the period are likewise now extinct. Among them were three species similar to the horse, two types of camels and a number of bovine creatures closely related to cows and buffalo.

Other archeological sites related to the Clovis people also have the remains of these and other animals, further adding to the conjecture that the Clovis were great hunters.

People who support the overkill theory argue that these animals could generally be considered "naïve," which means that, because they did not evolve on this continent with humans present, as occurred in Africa and Asia, they did not develop strategies to escape human predators. According to this theory, compared to their African and Asian cousins, humans in North America had a much easier time hunting their prey.

Under these conditions, it is speculated that humans were able to spread quickly across the continent and hunt and kill a large number of animals. They killed so many, especially the herbivores, that they drove them to extinction, it is alleged. And with many of the herbivores depleted, the animals that preyed on them, such as lions, tigers and bears (humans, too), suffered. Scavengers would also have found food to be scarce.

The fossil record for this period shows that a major extinction event occurred worldwide at this same time. Whether it was caused by overkill at the hands of humans is still being debated.

Wooly mammoths. These majestic creatures that once roamed North wAmerica became extinct.

The overkill argument goes on to state that in places where humans did not live, several forms of megafauna continued to flourish. For example, wooly mammoths survived on islands uninhabited by humans for hundreds of years after the last ice age. These mammoths became extinct only around 1700 BC, when humans first came to these islands. Supporters of the overkill hypothesis also assert that other areas, such as Australia, New Zealand and Madagascar, suffered similar extinctions of megafauna and other animals that coincided with the arrival of humans.

If this overkill theory represents reality, it supports the suggestion given earlier that the Clovis people created a situation that had pronounced effects on the continent and on the fate of their descendants several millennia later.

The Consequences of not Domesticating

At the time it is theorized humans first appeared on the American continents, there were a wide variety of animals that could have been domesticated by these humans as they evolved into more sophisticated societies. They include the three species of horses, two species of camels and the bovine-type creatures that became extinct. If these animals would have continued to exist alongside humans, there is little doubt that eventually people would have figured out a way to ride and domesticate them. And that would have had huge implications for the subsequent culture of the American peoples.

As things turned out, though, no culture in the Americas—be it one that built pyramids or one that remained nomadic—had any animal it could reasonably ride or use to transport materials. Some South American tribes had llamas as pack animals, but they couldn't really carry much. And they were not used as riding animals.

When the first Europeans arrived, the people of the Americas were stunned by the sight of humans astride the massive animals that we call horses. These animals allowed the Spaniards to travel much faster over the landscape, which assisted them in their efforts at conquest.

But the Spanish and other Europeans had help from smaller sources as well. If the overkill theory is true, then it explains why most Native American cultures had no real domesticated animals save for dogs, turkeys and llamas. The importance of this development cannot be understated.

Because Native Americans did not domesticate animals the same way Europeans and Asians did, they were not exposed to zoonotic diseases to anywhere near the same degree. Zoonotic diseases (either bacterial or viral) develop in animals (mostly) and then, through mutation and other means, can be transmitted to humans. Over 60 percent of all diseases are zoonotic in nature, and cultures that domesticate animals are exposed to more of them. Increased exposure to these diseases has a number of effects, both positive and negative.

On the negative side, plagues and epidemics easily spread through societies with domesticated animals. The Black Plague, which pervaded Europe in the 14th century, killing between one-quarter and one-third of the population, is the perfect example of a zoonotic disease. There is also evidence that smallpox, measles, diphtheria, HIV and influenza were also initially zoonotic diseases.

On the positive side, however, increased exposure to zoonotic diseases means that the society as a whole has greater immunity to such diseases. Yes, when the Black Plague swept through Europe, it did kill a lot of people. But Europe had been hit by many plagues in the centuries previous. As a result, some immunity was already built into the society, so not everyone who contracted the disease died. And many people didn't catch the plague at all. If it had been the first time Europe had been hit with a zoonotic disease, the story would have had a different ending.

Thus, when the Europeans first came to the Americas, they brought with them a number of zoonotic diseases, such as smallpox, tuberculosis, measles, anthrax and others, which had existed in their homelands for centuries. But in North America, because the Natives didn't have domesticated animals to the extent they had in Europe and Asia, they had little exposure to zoonotic diseases. And thus they had very little societal immunity to them.

As a result, millions upon millions of humans in North, South and Central America were infected and killed by diseases such as the ones mentioned above.

Archeological evidence shows over and over again that everywhere Europeans appeared for the first time in North America after Columbus, the local population of Natives plummeted in an extremely short period of time because of disease. The diseases that came from across the Atlantic showed no mercy.

Many scientists have noted that this epidemic of death was more severe than any other known disease outbreak in human history.

The Black Plague is considered one of the worst pandemics in the history of world. And rightly so. As noted earlier, more than one-third of Europe's population is believed to have been killed in this epidemic, which ran from 1347 to 1351. Estimates of the number of people killed range from 25 to 40 million. The pandemic also had enormous religious, economic and social repercussions at all levels of European society and culture. It took Europe more than 150 years to recover from the effects of the Black Plague.

There have been other major pandemics since then, including the Spanish flu epidemic after World War I, which claimed over 20 million lives. Currently, the HIV/AIDS epidemic has claimed more than 25 million lives worldwide since 1981, most of them in Africa.

The epidemic of disease that swept through the Americas after the arrival of the Europeans was of longer duration than the Black Plague, the Spanish flu epidemic and even HIV/AIDS.

And the overall impact was much more devastating. It claimed 90 percent of the population. Nearly every Native American at the time caught some sort of zoonotic disease and was killed by it.

Many highly respected archeologists, such as Timothy Pertulla of Austin, Texas; Patricia Galloway of the University of Texas; and Ann Ramenofsky of the University of New Mexico, have determined that the population of the Americas at the time before Columbus ranged from 80 to 100 million people, equal to the population of Europe at the time or higher.

Doing the calculation, if 90 percent of the 80 to 100 million people died during this epidemic, then you have a figure of 72 to 90 million people killed. On the low side of those figures, that means more than double the population of Canada today would have died of these imported diseases. On the high side, that's more than all the people killed, military and civilian, in World Wars I and II.

One can also look at these deaths from another angle. At the time these European diseases were sweeping through the Americas, the entire population of the world was estimated to be around 500 million people. Thus, if 72 to 90 million people were killed by disease, one out of every six or seven people in the entire world was killed by this epidemic. That's a staggering figure. Translated to today's world population, one-sixth or one-seventh of the population dying by disease would mean about one billion people. Even stretched out over a period of 50 years or a century, which was roughly the post-Columbus epidemic period, it would still be almost unimaginable. A billion people dead of disease over the course of 50 to 100 years translates to 10 to 20 million people dying every year.

If a pandemic of similar scale occurred in our time, that would equate to the entire population of Africa being wiped out. Or every single person in North, South and Central America wiped off the face of the planet. Which is pretty much what happened in the years after Columbus came to the New World.

It's no wonder that many Europeans arriving after the first wave of immigration to the New World found much of it to be an empty wilderness. Many of the inhabitants—the descendents of people who had lived there for thousands of years—were now dead.

This whole tragic situation can be attributed to pre-Columbian residents of the Americas not having been exposed to a wide range of zoonotic diseases, which, many scientists claim, was because the Clovis people were such great hunters. And one reason why they were great hunters was that they had developed that technological marvel of the time, the Clovis point.

But imagine a different scenario. Imagine, if you will, that the Clovis people did not develop such a point and did not cause the extinction of these animals. Then they may have developed cultures in which animals such as horses or camels were an important form of transportation. And they may have domesticated a variety of other large animals and been exposed to zoonotic diseases.

These diseases would probably have been different from the European ones. But even so, their exposure could have reduced the impact of the introduction of new diseases from Europe.

Even if they didn't have protection—and all those tens of millions of people died anyway—something else may have happened. The zoonotic diseases of the New World could have easily spread to the Old World, and the resulting epidemics could have had the same dramatic effect on Europe. Millions upon millions of Europeans could have been infected and killed by new diseases from the New World.

Such a situation would have changed the balance of the entire world, in an even greater variety of ways than what happened in reality. The societies and cultures of Europe and America could have both been dramatically reduced by their contact. With such a significant decrease in population in Europe, the Renaissance and the Age of Exploration may have been cut short before they fully blossomed. The Industrial Revolution may never have taken place, or it may have taken place somewhere else or at a much later date, such as now.

Muslim kings, some of whom had been recently kicked out of Spain, could have seen an opportunity to return. They could have waited for the effects of disease to fade and moved into a now-empty Europe the way Europeans spread throughout the Americas.

Or explorers from Asia could have arrived in Europe sometime after the epidemics had run their course and found the land mostly uninhabited. They could have set up colonies, imported settlers.

The world today could have been a completely different place.

It's fascinating to note how such an apparently small thing has the potential to change the world: how the development of a particular type of spearhead like the Clovis point over 12,000 years ago may have had such a huge effect on the state of the world, not just of 1492, but extending through the 21st century.

Other Possibilities

Still, the overkill theory is only a theory. Although there is ample evidence to back it up—and many scientists subscribe to it and all its repercussions—there are just as many experts who believe the Clovis people could not have driven so many animals in the Americas to the point of extinction.

Almost everyone agrees, though, that there was a Pleistocene Extinction Event, that a large number of animal species did die off around the same time the Clovis people started to fade from prehistory. The fossil record proves that a large percentage of animals in all parts of the world that weighed over 90 pounds became extinct around 10,000 years ago. In some areas, such as South America, almost every single animal over 220 pounds became extinct.

The reason many scientists believe humans were not the main cause of these extinctions is because this event occurred all over the world, not just in the Americas. The Clovis people, like many other humans in other parts of the globe, did not rely on animals as their primary source of food. The same sites that showed the Clovis to be great hunters also revealed that they had diverse diets.

Even though they were spread throughout the continent, the Clovis were extremely knowledgeable of the edible plants in whatever part of the continent they lived. And they made great use of these plants, fruits and nuts as food.

Also, although the Clovis may have lived in most parts of the continent, they did nevertheless live in small hunter-gatherer bands of 50 or fewer. And for these people to cause the extinction of so many animals, so much must have been wasted. But these Paleo-Indian cultures of this time, many scientists argue, were not the kind of people to waste so much meat. When they successfully hunted an animal, it is highly likely that they used almost every part of that animal, either as food or clothing or to create tools.

It should also be noted that some animals—such as the bison we see today that many Native groups were known to have hunted—did not become extinct the same way that other, similar animals did.

Some scientists claim there is a bit of a bias in the people who promote the overkill theory. In Europe, there was a similar extinction of both megafauna and smaller animals. There was also migration of humans into other parts of Europe, especially the more northern countries of Denmark and Scandinavia and the northern areas of Germany and France. These people were also great hunters. But the same scientists who blame the Clovis and other early Americans for the extinction of animals in America do not blame the European tribes for the extinction of similar animals on that continent.

Scientists offer other explanations for the European extinction. Climate change, for one. And that is the other theory that many experts use to explain the extinction of large animals in North America. Something occurred in the climate that caused certain animals to die off, while others thrived, they explain.

Some scientists say that the overall temperature of the world rose, which made life more difficult for much larger animals that had evolved to survive in ice-age climates. Another group blames a meteorite strike, similar to what occurred around the time of the demise of the dinosaurs. There have been at least six possible meteorite strike sites found in North America, plus a number in Greenland. The meteorite theory states that the impact of the meteorite threw up a massive cloud of dust that blocked a significant amount of sunlight for many years, thereby cooling the planet. Although the animals were able to survive the cold, many of the plants did not, the theory continues, so the herbivores lost much of their food supply and began to die out. And as the herbivores died, so did the animals that preyed on them.

Because this meteorite strike occurred in the Northern Hemisphere, the prevailing air currents would have distributed the dust throughout the hemisphere but not so much southward, so it would have been the northern areas that suffered more extinctions. This explains why Africa and southern Asia still have large land animals—such as elephants and rhinos—whereas North America, Europe and parts of northern Asia lost most of theirs.

Still, just as with the human overkill theory, there are many arguments against the ones involving climate change. The possible reasons and theories behind the Pleistocene Extinction Event are varied and hotly contested. Why exactly it happened is considered to be an extremely controversial subject in the scientific community.

Some truths remain: the Clovis did exist. And with their great hunting skills and development of the Clovis point, they did spread throughout North America. And they are the ancestors of almost every single indigenous group living in North and South America today.

But were they the first? Were they the original group to migrate into the Americas, across the Bering land bridge, through the gap in the ice, across the continent and farther south? Was anyone in the Americas before the Clovis?

As more and more archaeologists study the prehistory of the Americas and its people, and as they unearth additional sites in other parts of these huge continents, more and more people are wondering the same thing.

Chapter Five

Before Clovis

In 1975, a veterinary student was hiking in the Monte Verde area of Chile. It's in the southern part of the country, in the region known as Patagonia, a 400,000-square-mile tract of land that makes up the most southerly section of South America. As a result of overly intensive logging, the land in Monte Verde was becoming heavily eroded in places.

As the student made his way around the area, he spotted what initially looked to be the bone of a cow protruding from the bed of Chinchihuapi Creek. However, it was unusual enough that he felt compelled to alert archeologists at the Southern University of Chile about his find. Two professors, Mario Pino and Tom Dillehay, made their way to the site and determined that the "cow bone" was actually part of a mastodon. Intrigued by this find, they started excavating the site in 1977. For years, the team worked diligently on the site. They then spent two years writing a two-volume book outlining their discoveries and released it in 1987. What they had found was astonishing.

A sample of a fossil mastodon skull. The Clovis people were adept at hunting animals as large as this.

They determined that the bones of that mastodon were actually the remains of a hunt, and that the site was actually an ancient village of about 20 to 30 people. The long-ago inhabitants had built a 20-foot-long, tent-like structure at the edge of the creek. It had been constructed of long poles and animal hides. Inside the main structure, poles and hides had been arranged to split the area into separate quarters. Each section had its own brazier or cooking pit.

There were also two other hearth-like structures outside the main tent, plus a wide variety of tools scattered throughout the entire area. And because of the way the area was preserved, there were many remnants of berries, nuts, seeds and other foods, plus an imprint of a child's foot and some fossilized human dung.

With its impressive preservation and range of artifacts, the Monte Verde site was already an incredible find. But when Pino and Dillehay began to carbon date the artifacts on the site, they were incredulous.

Almost every single piece that they had found, removed and catalogued during the eight years of excavation dated to almost 15,000 years ago. This meant that the people who had lived on this site had been there over 1000 years before the Clovis culture had flourished. And because Monte Verde is in one of the most southerly parts of the Americas, it was presumed that the ancestors of these people would have had to have crossed the Bering Strait land bridge even earlier.

This information meant that the arrival of these people pre-dated the era of the Clovis people by more than 2000 years, the same amount of time between the birth of Christ and today. Not much time in a geological sense but, from a human point of view, a very long time.

It was a stunning revelation to the archeological world that sparked massive debates. Like the discovery 50 years earlier of the site in Clovis, New Mexico, it forced people to rethink their accepted theories of how and when humans arrived in the Americas. Over time, the idea that Monte Verde was the oldest site of human habitation in the Americas slowly gained acceptance.

Although a number of scholars still maintain that the Clovis people were the first humans in the Americas, the evidence of Monte Verde is too overwhelming to dismiss.

One of the key questions that the Monte Verde discovery brought up was how did they get there? Did they walk there, moving southward generation after generation so that, after 1000 years, they finally reached Monte Verde? And, if so, how?

It is true that the Bering land bridge, Beringia, did exist at the time, so it would have been possible for the ancestors of these people to cross over by that route. But massive glaciers covered most of the northern parts of North America. Crossing these immense glaciers would have been tremendously difficult even today with our modern vehicles, freeze-dried food, GPS and tents and sleeping bags rated to −40 degree temperatures. So how could these relatively primitive people cross an icebound landscape thousands of miles long?

Maybe they didn't come by land.

As early as 1787, some researchers have suggested that these people arrived by sea, crossing the Pacific slowly, island by island, the way Polynesians traveled and colonized Hawaii and Rapa Nui (also known as Easter Island). This is a fanciful thought, conjuring up images of great sea voyages made in small, yet sturdy boats. In 1999, a modern expedition of boats made in the Polynesian style crossed over 2000 miles of the Pacific Ocean, from the Gambier Islands of French Polynesia to Rapa Nui, in 19 days.

If people could have crossed the 2000 miles to Rapa Nui, then it's plausible, it was suggested, that people could have crossed the remaining 3000 miles to continental Chile. Although such a trip could indeed have been possible, studies have shown that Rapa Nui was first colonized somewhere between 400 and 700 AD, or about 1300 to 1600 years ago.

Recall, however, that the Monte Verde site is over 10 times older than the colonization of Rapa Nui. Even so, there are those who say that some cultural and genetic similarities exist between Australian aborigines and certain tribes of Patagonia. And given that the first Australians have been shown to have migrated from Southeast Asia, through the islands of the Malay Archipelago, it is speculated that they could have continued eastward, island-hopping across the Pacific until they reached South America. One recent study claimed that the DNA in a type of South American chicken indicated the animal was descended from a Polynesian chicken, thus proving a pre-Columbian connection from across the Pacific. However, the study was later refuted.

Nevertheless, it is interesting to note that Chilean students are taught both the Pacific crossing origin model and the Beringia land bridge origin model of human arrival in the Americas.

Still, a growing number of people are considering the possibility that some of the first peoples to reach the Americas did arrive by boat. Except that in this new theory, they didn't cross the Pacific; they just traveled around the edges, making their way along the shorelines of Asia and Beringia, down the coast of present-day Canada and farther.

"There was boat use in Japan 20,000 years ago," according to anthropologist Jon Erlandson at the University of Oregon.

"The Kurile Islands [north of Japan] are like stepping stones to Beringia," he explained. "Migrants could have then skirted the tidewater glaciers in Canada right on down the coast."

This tactic would have been possible because, despite the ice age, many tidewater areas would have remained free of ice. And these areas would have been abundant with marine life and edible coastal plants. A marine-based culture with a diet based on fish, sea mammals and coastal plants could have moved relatively easily across from Asia and dispersed southward, spreading down the West Coast the same way the Clovis people are believed to have spread throughout North America.

The difficulty in finding actual evidence for this theory is that, after the ice age ended and the glaciers retreated, many of these previously exposed coastlines would have been flooded. The remains of settlements of any type would today be deep underwater. Finding such sites would be extremely difficult and expensive, excavating and then studying them almost impossible. So there isn't enough archeological proof to convince the scientific establishment. Of course, this same scientific establishment at one time didn't believe that humans lived in North America more than 8000 years ago, and they were proven wrong on that point.

Nevertheless, the Pacific coast migration is an intriguing concept that isn't easily dismissed. Many North American coastal cultures—such as the Haida, the Inuit, the Dorset and the Thule—were quite adept at building watercraft.

For thousands of years, the northern peoples of the Western Hemisphere have explored coves and bays and traveled great expanses of water from the west coast of Alaska to the east coast of Greenland. To do so, they used a highly versatile and nimble craft that is now known and used throughout the world: the kayak.

Chapter Six

The Kayak

Brigit Fischer was born February 25, 1962, in Brandenburg an der Havel, an East German city of about 80,000 people. Before World War II, the city was known for its bicycle and toy factories.

At the time Brigit was growing up, East Germany was keen to make an international name for itself in sport. Scouts traveled the country, looking for children who showed skill, talent or aptitude in sporting activities. Brigit was one of those children. She attended an army boarding school for athletes and over time would become one of the greatest German athletes in its history, male or female.

Brigit won her first gold medal for East Germany at the Moscow Summer Olympics in 1980. She was only 18 years old and was the youngest gold medal winner in her sport. She went on to win a total of eight gold medals and four silvers over six Olympics, the last medal in 2004 when she was 42 years old. She is one of the greatest Olympians in the history of the Games, tied in fifth place for the most gold medals won by any athlete and in second place for the most gold medals won by a woman.

Brigit Fischer's sport is officially called Olympic Canoeing, but most people call it kayaking. To clarify the issue, canoes and kayaks have many similarities but also some key differences. Kayaks sit much lower in the water but at the same time have less drag, so it doesn't take as much force to move them forward. Because kayaks sit lower in the water, they have a lower center of balance. Therefore, one sits to paddle a kayak, instead of kneeling, as in a canoe. Two further differences are that typically, kayaks have closed tops whereas canoes are open, and kayak paddles are double-ended, whereas canoe paddles have a single blade. And most modern kayaks have a rudder, which is used to turn the boat through the use of foot pedals, but canoes do not.

Origins of the Kayak

Kayaking didn't start out as a sporting event. Kayaks have been in use for at least 4000 years, and they may have been around much longer. They were first used by people of the North American Arctic—the Inuit, the Aleuts and the now extinct Dorset and Thule people—as a form of transportation, mostly for hunting.

Kayaks were great for hunting because they were fast, easily maneuverable and low to the water. Hunters used kayaks to sneak up on a variety of sea mammals, from seals to whales. They draped a piece of sealskin over the front of their kayak and themselves as camouflage. To animals such as seals, the camouflaged craft looked like another seal or even a piece of drifting ice. It took a lot of skill for a hunter to slowly move close enough so he could harpoon a seal. Imagine the skill and strength needed to harpoon and then capture a whale, even a small one. Imagine the fortitude needed to paddle the kayak so that a hunter—or even a group of hunters—could bring the slain whale back to the settlement.

Today we have mass production and fiberglass and plastics technologies, but kayak construction was originally quite different for the people of the North. In the Inuit language, the word *kayak* (or *qajak*) means "hunter's boat." Traditionally, each and every kayak was personally built by the person who would use it.

In many cases, a builder determined the size of his kayak based on his own body measurements. The length was three spans of the hunter's outstretched arms. The width at its largest was the width of the hunter's hips plus two of his fists. And the depth of the kayak was the hunter's fist with the thumb extended. On average, a kayak was about 17 feet long, 21 inches wide and seven inches deep.

The frame of the kayak was mostly wood, but because the Arctic is almost devoid of trees, the hunter had to rely on driftwood that washed up from the cold Arctic Ocean or wood from trees that had fallen into rivers much farther south and then drifted northward with the current. If there wasn't enough driftwood around, the bones or antlers of caribou would suffice. Even whalebone was used if better materials weren't available.

One must remember that the northern Natives didn't have any metal nails to pound the sections together. A combination of sealskin rope and caribou sinew was used to lash the individual pieces of wood together to form the complete frame.

A cluster of kayaks in Noatak, Alaska. Kayaks were traditionally made from sealskin and driftwood and/or bone.

Once the frame was finished, the hunter and his wife worked together to create the skin that covered the kayak. Sealskin was the primary choice because of its wide availability. To make the skins pliable to mold around the frame, they were placed in hot water. They were then removed and, while still hot, the hair was scraped away. The skins were then placed in a sealskin bag and packed in with some seal fat to keep them flexible and easy to use.

When enough skins had been prepared, they were stretched over the frame and stitched together using sinew and sealskin rope. The entire boat was then wrapped with caribou sinew and left to dry. As it dried, the sealskin covering would contract and slowly form a tight and almost waterproof cover around the frame. The skin was then sewn to the frame using caribou sinew. To further improve the water-resistant nature of the kayak, each seam was rinsed in seawater. The hunter then placed additional pieces of sealskin inside the kayak to form another protective layer.

The paddles were also made of found wood and were long and much thinner than the kayak paddles seen today.

Natives across the Arctic all made kayaks, but their designs differed from group to group. The Aleuts who lived on the west coast of Alaska and along the Aleutian Islands preferred a much bigger design known as a baidarka. An older design, it came across the Bering Strait from Siberia, where it is still made. A much longer boat than a typical kayak, a baidarka could sometimes seat two or three individuals and featured a forked bow. Baidarkas were built in the same way as other kayaks. Interestingly, the hunters who built them thought of them as living creatures.

The Inuit and the West Greenland Natives built and used the more traditional single-person craft. East Greenland kayaks were similar but were built to be more snug to the hunter and featured higher bows and sterns to improve maneuverability.

Kayaks could be used for short voyages or long ones. But not too long. They were mostly hunting boats. If there was a need for a boat to move from one seasonal settlement to another, the people built a boat called an umiak. An umiak was a longer, open boat that could carry many individuals at once along with dogs and materials such as food, tents, sealskin and so on. This boat could be paddled, or, if needed, a sealskin sail could be attached to a small mast. Women did most of the paddling on an umiak, which is why it is called the "women's boat."

Even though kayaks were generally used for short trips, there are many reports of long voyages taken with kayaks. By the end of the 17th century, three kayaks had been found in various coastline locations of Scotland. One of them was found near Aberdeen with the barely alive Inuit paddler still inside. He later died, but his kayak is still preserved at the Marischal Museum in Aberdeen.

The Kayak Comes to Europe

The kayak initially came to the attention of Europeans following some of the first Arctic explorations from that continent. Sailors and explorers appreciated the unusual and simple design of the kayak. It took them a while to figure out the dimensions and how to make the sealskin watertight, but they finally succeeded. Many of these returning sailors recreated these crafts, which they called "canoes" at the time, and paddled the rivers and lakes of their home countries.

Scottish explorer John MacGregor is credited with popularizing the kayak, or "canoe" as he called it, in England and other parts of Europe. His interest in the craft began in 1858, when he was introduced to kayaking during a trip to Canada and the United States. The son of a general, he had been a champion marksman, but an accident on a railroad left him without the ability to aim accurately. So he turned to kayaking.

MacGregor built his own kayaks. The first and best known was an 80-pound, 15-foot model covered with rubberized canvas. He named it *Rob Roy*, after the famed Scottish hero, who was also a distant relative. MacGregor started paddling up and down the Thames River in England, crossed the English Channel a number of times, continued on to Europe and through its many riverways and lakes, up through the Baltics and during one trip, through the Middle East.

His book, *A Thousand Miles in a Rob Roy Canoe*, was an international bestseller, making MacGregor a relatively wealthy man for his time.

Once kayaks became known in Europe, some European kayakers used them to travel long distances, like the Natives of the Arctic sometimes did. For example, German-born Franz Romer paddled and sailed his wood-frame kayak from Lisbon, Portugal, to Puerto Rico in 1928. It took him 58 days. And the most difficult part of this trip probably wasn't the distance he had to travel, but how he had to do it. Because Romer was traveling by himself with no support except what he could catch along the way, his kayak was packed tight with food and other supplies. Therefore, for the first few weeks, Romer had to keep his legs squeezed in place, until he ate through some of his supplies. And because he wasn't able to stretch out for those first weeks, he suffered from severe boils and atrophy of his legs. After making landfall, he was intent on making it to New York, so after some weeks of rest and recuperation, he went north from Puerto Rico. Unfortunately, he headed directly into the eye of a hurricane and was never heard from again.

The Kayak in Wartime

In Europe, kayaks remained homemade recreational marine craft for a number of years. But even the military could see their usefulness for stealth operations. During World War II, the British established an elite commando unit called the Royal Marines Boom Patrol Detachment.

This unit used kayaks on a number of raiding missions, including the famed Operation Frankton. In this 1942 commando raid, a group of Royal Marines and their kayaks were taken by submarine to an estuary near the French city of Bordeaux. At the time, Bordeaux was occupied by the Germans, who were using it as a key port for supplies shipped from other parts of the world. At the time of the raid, the Germans had many fully loaded supply ships waiting at Bordeaux. They contained valuable items such as oil, crude rubber and other raw materials that could be used to make weapons, munitions, military vehicles and other devices important to the German war machine.

To deprive the enemy of these materials, it was determined that 13 men could paddle a few kayaks up the estuary to Bordeaux, plant mines on a number of ships to destroy them and then escape southward through Spain. The marines paddled by night and hid in quiet coves during the day, hoping to evade the 30-plus ships that patrolled the area.

On the first night, two kayaks and four men were lost to high seas. After regrouping, the remaining kayaks managed to slip by three German frigates. When morning broke, one kayak and its two occupants were captured; the two soldiers were later shot as spies by the Germans.

On the second night, the commandoes with the two remaining kayaks paddled 22 miles. On night three, it was 15 miles. During the fourth night, the flow of the tide held them to only nine miles. On the fifth night, they split up, and, in a scene reminiscent of a Hollywood thriller, they slowly and quietly moved throughout the port, from ship to ship, striving to evade the roving searchlights. In total, they managed to plant a series of mines on a total of five ships, despite almost being detected a number of times.

By pure luck, the two groups met along a river as they were paddling away. They paddled together until morning. After sinking their kayaks, they split up and continued southward. Two days later, two men were captured, interrogated and then shot by the Germans.

The other two were also considered lost, but, two months later, in late February, the French Resistance contacted the Allies, saying they had the surviving two soldiers. A week later, they were back in England after traveling through Spain and flying in from Gibraltar.

In all, the raid damaged five ships and their cargo, an act that Winston Churchill believed shortened the war by six months.

Kayaks continued to be of wooden construction until the 1950s. Then fiberglass boats were introduced in the United States, with inflatable ones being more popular in Europe. Molded plastic kayaks entered production in the '70s, thereby allowing for stronger and lighter craft.

Nowadays, there are more than 13 different forms of kayak sport and recreation, from whitewater to sea kayaking to surf kayaking. Kayaking is one of the fastest growing watercraft and paddling recreation sports. According to the Chicago-based National Marine Manufacturers Association, over 350,000 kayaks are sold every year. In a strange bit of trivia, a few years ago, the sales of kayaks in Canada surpassed the sales of the traditional Canadian canoe.

And although the use of kayaks in Operation Frankton was credited with shortening World War II, this was not the only Native American contribution to the war effort.

Chapter Seven

Code Talkers

War in the Pacific

On December 7, 1941, "a date that will live in infamy," the Empire of Japan attacked Pearl Harbor. Called "Operation Z" by the Japanese, the attack was designed as a preemptive strike to prevent the United States from interfering in Japan's plans for military action in other parts of the Pacific and Southeast Asia.

The attack had a devastating effect on the U.S. fleet in Hawaii, sinking or seriously damaged 18 ships, destroying 188 aircraft, killing almost 3000 Americans and wounding 1200 more.

Prior to the attack, the U.S. had resisted participation in the war that was spreading through Europe and the Pacific. But the attack on Pearl Harbor angered and galvanized the American populace. Within a day, the United States declared war on Japan. Because Japan was allied with German and Italy, those countries responded by declaring war on the United States. In the space of a few days, the United States became an official combatant in World War II.

Native Americans Enlist

Reaction from the American people was immediate. Many young men signed up to fight for their country. Native Americans were no exception, save for the enthusiasm to defend their country. Even though humorist (and Oklahoma Cherokee) Will Rogers once joked, "The United States never broke a treaty with a foreign government and never kept one with the Indians," Native Americans volunteered in droves.

Over 44,000 Natives signed up to serve for the United States in the war against the Axis powers of Japan, Germany and Italy. In many Native nations, almost every man old enough to serve voluntarily enlisted, some of them standing in line for hours at a recruitment office, rifles in hand, ready to fight. Nearly one-fourth of the Mescalero Apaches in New Mexico voluntarily enlisted. Nearly all the eligible male Chippewas at the Grand Portage Reservation did the same. The story repeated itself over and over across the United States, from reservation to reservation and even to the cities where a large number of Native Americans lived off-reservation.

The number of Native Americans enlisting to fight in World War II was equivalent to one-third of all Native American males between the ages of 18 and 50. It is estimated that over 90 percent of Native Americans who served in the war joined voluntarily. No other group of Americans voluntarily enlisted at that rate. If all Americans had enlisted at the same rate as Native Americans, there would have been no need to implement the draft.

Most Native American nations scoffed at such a draft, some even finding it insulting to be conscripted. "Since when," a member of the Blackfeet Nation said, "has it been necessary for Blackfeet to draw lots to fight?"

The Iroquois Nation had no need to declare war on Germany because it was technically still at war with that country. During World War I, the Iroquois, as a nation expressing its independence, had declared war on Germany. And because they had not been included in the peace talks after World War I ended, they just renewed their declaration.

Native American soldiers fought on all fronts and in all the military campaigns in which the United States participated, from Africa to Italy, from Normandy on D-Day to Iwo Jima and all the islands in the Pacific where battles took place. There were heroes, great sacrifices and winners of medals, too many to be listed here.

On the home front, Native Americans also responded. Even though they were at the low end of the economic scale, Native Americans bought war bonds (over $50 million by 1944) and donated to groups such as the Red Cross and others at unprecedented rates. As well, over 150,000 Native Americans directly participated in civilian and military aspects of the American war effort.

"A good deal of credit must go to the Native Americans for their outstanding part in America's victory in World War II," wrote Lieutenant Colonel Thomas D. Morgan (Ret.), a military operations analyst.

They sacrificed more than most—both individually and as a group. They left the land they knew to travel to strange places, where people did not always understand their ways. They had to forego the dances and rituals that were an important part of their life. They had to learn to work under non-Indian supervisors in situations that were wholly new to them. It was a tremendously diffi-cult adjustment; more than for white America, which had known modern war and mobilization before. But in the process, Native Americans became Indian-Americans, not just American Indians.

In Canada, although First Nations peoples were exempt from conscription because of a stipulation in earlier treaties that stated they did not have to fight in wars involving the British, over 3000 Aboriginal Canadians enlisted. Like their American counterparts, they participated in every single battle and front in which Canada participated, including the defense of Hong Kong. Over 200 Aboriginal Canadians were killed in World War II, and 18 medals of bravery were awarded.

Keeping It Secret

Although Native Americans played a variety of roles in the battles against the Axis powers of Germany, Italy and Japan, one of the most interesting dealt with the development of codes. During the battle of the Pacific, the United States used Navajo soldiers as "code talkers" whose primary job was the transmission of secret tacti-cal messages. Code talkers transmitted these messages over military telephone or radio communications using codes built upon their Native languages.

Having Native Americans use the unique properties of their language to pass on orders, reports and other secret mes-sages was not an idea original to World War II, however.

The original code talkers, the Choctaw coders from World War I

During World War I, U.S. colonel A.W. Bloor noticed that he had a large number of Native Americans, mostly Choctaws from southeastern Oklahoma, serving in his 142nd Infantry. Bloor observed that when two of these soldiers wanted to share something private between themselves without the other soldiers understanding them, they spoke in their Native tongue.

One day he devised an experiment. On October 28, 1918, two companies of the 2nd Battalion were supposed to withdraw from the French village of Chufilly to Chardeny. Bloor wanted to ensure that the order to withdraw made it to the soldiers without the Germans learning of their plans in advance. Both sides had put a lot of effort into intercepting the orders and commands that flowed between the various posts. Codes were constantly used, implementing various mathematical formulas as well as language and word tricks, to confuse the other side.

Both sides had great mathematicians and a thorough knowledge of the each other's language, including the various quirks and the usage of slang and dialects. As a result, for the most part, all codes were eventually broken. An additional problem was that the codes tended to become so complex and confusing that it took a long time to decode messages that were sent between friendly troops. During times of war, however, speed was of the essence.

Thus, for the withdrawal of troops on this late October day, Colonel Bloor decided to use his Choctaw speakers to pass on the orders. The ploy worked, and the 2nd Battalion of the 142nd Infantry successfully withdrew from their position. The Germans were caught completely off guard by the movement, even though they had intercepted the radio message that had included the order. One captured German officer admitted that they were completely confused by the use of the Choctaw language.

Following this success, an elite group of Choctaw-speaking soldiers was established as code talkers during World War I. Although the squadron was small, they were highly successful in transmitting orders between various battle groups and battalions.

The Choctaw code talkers of World War I were so successful and feared by the Germans that during the buildup of their military in the 1930s, Adolph Hitler himself ordered that the German army prepare themselves. He sent over 30 anthropologists to the United States so they could study and learn as many American Native languages as possible.

Even so, because of the diversity of the languages and the many dialects, the Germans did not succeed. The Americans were aware of the German initiative and, as a result, did not implement large-scale Native American code-talking programs for the war in Europe.

Nevertheless, a group of 14 Comanche soldiers did act as code talkers during the invasion of Normandy on D-Day. And they continued to operate in Europe throughout the rest of the war. In 1989, the government of France awarded the Comanche code talkers the Chevalier of the National Order of Merit.

In the Pacific Theatre, the Americans were having a difficult time with their codes. Because Japan had at its disposal a large selection of fluent English speakers as well as some skilled cryptanalysts, every single code the U.S. developed in the early parts of the war was broken by the Japanese. At the same time, the Japanese also managed to sabotage some of these codes and use them against the Americans by planting false orders and movements of troops and ships.

In response, the U.S. developed even more complex codes, but they became more unwieldy as time wore on. The more complex the code, the more difficult it was for the recipient to decipher the message that was transmitted. During the battle for Guadalcanal, for example, some codes were so complex that it took over two and a half hours just to decipher a simple message.

Let's Try Navajo

Philip Johnson was a civilian engineer who had been hired by the water department of the City of Los Angeles prior to World War II. As a younger man, he had served in World War I, and it's likely that during this time he had seen the work of the Choctaw code talkers.

Johnson was the son of a missionary who had been allowed to establish a Christian mission near the Navajo Reservation in Arizona. As a result, Johnson had grown up with many Navajo friends and had become relatively fluent in their language. After the attack on Pearl Harbor, he realized that there was an opportunity to use code talkers in this new war.

The Navajo language was ideal for this purpose because it had a complex grammar and was an unwritten language. At the time of World War II, nothing had been published—no books, no articles—using the Navajo language. Also, its syntax and tonal qualities were very complex, to the point that it was almost unintelligible to outsiders. In fact, when the war began, Johnson was one of only 30 non-Navajo people (none of them Japanese) who could speak and understand the language. Also, the way he spoke and used the language, even with his years of practice, made it very obvious to the Navajo that he was not a Native speaker.

Johnson first presented his idea to the United States Marines with the help of four Navajos who worked for the City of Los Angeles. Using a series of tests under simulated combat conditions, Johnson and the four Navajos showed that they could transmit and receive, code and decode a series of three-line messages. Each message would take them only about 20 seconds, compared to the 30 minutes it took a code machine to do the same thing.

Impressed by this demonstration, the United States Marines approved the Navajo Code Talker Program, and the first 29 Navajos were recruited. These soldiers developed the original code of 200 words, using uniquely formal descriptive nomenclatures in Navajo—such as the word "tortoise" to refer to a tank or "potato" to refer to a grenade—in the code. Several of these terms, such as "gofasters" for running shoes and "ink sticks" for pens, are still part of the informal vocabulary of the United States Marine Corps.

A codebook was developed, but it was never taken into the field for fear of it falling into enemy hands. Thus, the code talkers had to memorize the entire book and the variant uses of words and phrases so they could make themselves understandable to each other during combat situations.

In the first years of the war, over 200 Navajos were recruited for the code talker program, trained in the code and then sent out to Marine units throughout the Pacific. Many of these code talkers were just boys, some as young as 15 (although some as old as 35 were also recruited). For most, it was the first time that they had ever left home.

Although the Marines were skeptical of the Navajo code talkers at first, it didn't take long for the Natives to show their worth. During the battle of Iwo Jima, three Navajo code talkers worked around the clock during the first 48 hours of the battle and transmitted, received, coded and decoded over 800 messages, without a single mistake in any of them.

The Japanese had no idea how to deal with the Navajo code. It was unlike anything they had ever heard before. They tried every tactic they could and even forced a captured Navajo sergeant to intercept and interpret the messages. Although he was Navajo, he had not been part of the code talker training and was unable to understand the messages. Some Japanese heads literally rolled because they were unable to break this code.

By the war's end, over 400 Navajo code talkers had been recruited and deployed into combat. They served in every battle in the Pacific Theatre from 1942 to 1945. Their presence and work in battle allowed the U.S. Marines to communicate quickly, clearly and correctly. Many military experts say that the presence and the work of the Navajo code talkers played an integral part of the United States war effort. They also say that many key battles—such as Guadalcanal, Iwo Jima, Tarawa, Guam, the Marshall Islands, Midway and Peleliu, all major turning points in the fight against the Japanese—would have had different outcomes if not for the work of the Navajo code talkers.

At the end of the war, the Navajo code talkers went back to the U.S., unable to talk about what they had done or had exactly accomplished in the war. Many of them had no idea of their own contribution, because the code talker program was so secret. They knew they had served in the war and transmitted code, but they had no view of the big picture and the overall contribution they had made to the war effort.

The Navajo code was so successful—it was the only U.S. code that the Japanese did not break during World War II—that the Americans didn't want anyone else to know that it existed. It was used again during the Korean War and, up to 1968, during the Vietnam War. The project was declassified in 1968, but it still took until December 21, 2000, for 29 code talkers to be awarded the Congressional Gold Medal. Then, in 2007, the State of Texas posthumously awarded the Texas Medal of Honor to the 18 Choctaw code talkers who had served in World War I.

The Congressional gold medal that was awarded in 2000 to the surviving World War II Navajo code talkers

A monument to the Navajo code talkers was built in Window Rock, Arizona.

But again, this was not the first time that a contribution from the Natives of the Americas had played a major role in a war.

Chapter Eight

The Potato

The Potato War

The Potato War of 1778–79 was a short and relatively less damaging war compared to many of its era, but many historians declare that it was a turning point in European warfare.

Also called the War of Bavarian Succession, the Potato War was in its essence a battle between German-speaking states to determine which family or person would assume the leadership of the Duchy of Bavaria. There weren't many huge battles in this war, and most of the conflicts could be defined as minor skirmishes in which a few hundred soldiers were killed in actual warfare. But several thousands soldiers and civilians did die in this war because of starvation and disease brought about by starvation.

The Potato War ended not with a decisive battle but with an armistice agreement. Despite this ending, the war resulted in a high number of deaths and solved little or nothing.

Military commanders and leaders of the time saw these failings and determined that this old style of warfare—"cabinet warfare," in which diplomats hurried back and forth between the quarrelling monarchs or nobles, while relatively small battles continued in their useless yet destructive fashion—should be retired. As a result, the Potato War became the last war of this type in European history. The wars that followed this one, especially the Napoleonic Wars, were much different in that military tactics and strategy played a larger role in the outcome of the war than did diplomatic efforts.

The other difference between this war and others fought earlier is that instead of attacking each other, the opposing armies spent a lot of time in the early part of the war destroying crops to prevent the other side from replenishing their food supplies. The problem with this strategy was that as the war drew on and winter set in, there were no crops for either side to replenish their food supplies. And that is why this war is called the Potato War—because throughout this part of Germany, the most popular crop was the potato. But the tuber's popularity was only a recent development.

Early Uses of the Humble Potato

So ubiquitous is the potato—seemingly everywhere in the world, and so much a part of the cultural and culinary milieu of so many societies—that it seems it must have been found worldwide since the beginning of time. Called "the common root for the common man" by one writer, the potato was assumed by many people to have been a universal, wide-reaching plant since human beings first stood upright.

Siwash (Salishan) Indians digging potatoes in Washington State

But that is not the case. It seems almost unfathomable to us in the 21st century world that, prior to the arrival of Columbus and the rest of the Europeans in the "New World," no one outside of the Americas had ever seen or heard of the plant. Before 1492, no one in Europe, no one in India, no one in China—areas where potatoes are now among the most popular food items—had ever eaten a potato. Nor had they even realized that such a useful and nutritional plant existed.

Potatoes are truly one of the great gifts to the world from the American indigenous people.

Potatoes are members of the Solanaceae family of plants (also known as nightshades), which includes species such as belladonna, mandrake, capsicums, tomatoes, eggplants, tobacco and petunias. Many of these plants are originally native to the Americas. The common potato, which comes in many varieties, is scientifically known as *Solanum tuberosum*.

For thousands of years, a large number of ancient peoples throughout the Americas gathered various kinds of wild potatoes as food. For a long time, though, they did not cultivate potatoes. With wild potatoes so plentiful, there seemed no need to plant and care for them as an agricultural crop.

By 3000 BC, however, potatoes were being cultivated in Peru. Over time, they became the staple food for the Inca Empire. Potatoes were ideal, because the ancestors of the Incas had developed a means of ensuring their potatoes would last for a very long time, even years. The process turns potatoes into *chuños*; the term comes from a Quechua word that translates simply into "frozen potato."

The process of turning potatoes into chuños is a five-day operation, mostly involving exposing the mature tubers (the root of the plant that one eats) to the very cold nights of the Andean Altiplano (the high plains of South America near the Andes Mountains). During the day, the potatoes are exposed to the bright sun. After the third night of freezing, they are trampled underfoot. This part of the process extracts most of the moisture from the potatoes as well as removes the skins. The potatoes are left out for two more cold nights before becoming chuños.

There are two types of chuños. Black ones are the result of the basic chuño-making process. White ones are created by washing the potatoes after freezing them, usually by leaving them in a pool of water near a river for a period of time, and then drying them in the sun.

Chuños can be utilized in a wide variety of ways: in soups, stews, boiled, mashed, as a dessert or turned into flour suitable for making a number of different types of bread. They were and are still a popular food item in South America. Because of the tuber's versatility, the techniques for growing and using potatoes spread throughout the Americas. Many Native societies soon became potato growers and continued to grow them for centuries.

The Potato Feeds Europe

Once the Spanish started to spread throughout the Americas following the arrival of Christopher Columbus in 1492, the potato came to the attention of the Europeans. By this time, a diet heavy in potatoes was a feature not just of the Incas but had caught on with many of the other Native groups throughout the areas of the Americas where the Spanish explored and conquered.

Spanish sailors quickly realized the storage potential of the potato. They also found that these roots could be cooked in a numerous ways and provided good nutritional value on long sea voyages between Spain and New Spain (their North American lands). These new menu items were considered better than the basic gruel and other types of terrible food the early sailors consumed on their voyages.

The Spanish also spread potatoes into Italy during their normal trade relations. And because the climate wasn't as dry, potatoes grew better in Italy than in Spain.

Then, in 1567, a group of Dutch nobles decided to take a stand against the rule of the Spanish in the Netherlands. Phillip II, whose kingdom included the area now known as the Netherlands, was also the son of Charles V, the emperor of Spain. The Dutch nobles were incensed by the high taxes they had to pay to Phillip and, indirectly, to Spain, so they launched a revolt, which became known as the Eighty Years' War.

As part of their battle plan, the Dutch revolutionaries established a navy of privateers, known as the Sea Beggars, who preyed on Spanish ships. Over time, it became very difficult for the Spanish to transport soldiers by sea to the Netherlands. Instead, they went first to Italy by sea and then traversed the Alps through parts of France, Germany, Luxembourg and Belgium. One of their key foods for the trips was this new crop from the Americas, potatoes.

As the peasants and farmers in the path of the Spanish army discovered this new food, the potato began its spread throughout the area, even though most people of the time weren't keen on adopting a new food or planting something new in their fields and gardens. There were always fears that a strange new food, no matter how tempting, could carry disease. Indeed, when potatoes first came on the scene in Europe, there was a widespread belief that they could cause leprosy. These claims were so strong that certain French provincial governments passed laws banning the cultivation of potatoes.

But despite these worries, potatoes caught on relatively quickly for a newly introduced crop. The peasants adopted potatoes as a key food for a wide range of reasons. One was that the edible bits were underground. Therefore, it was difficult for marauding armies to pillage them when compared to aboveground crops such as grains. And even if the soldiers were hungry enough to dig for the potatoes, they never had the strength or the time to take all of them, the way they used to steal all the grain. So there were always enough potatoes left to sustain the members of the peasant farm.

In addition, a peasant family could raise enough potatoes in a fairly small space to feed their entire family for a year while also feeding a cow for milk and a couple of pigs to sell or to slaughter for meat. Compared to many crops of the time, potatoes were extremely suitable to the European diet and political systems because a large amount could be grown in a relatively short period of time. They also provided enough nutritional value and food bulk to keep a peasant family from starving and could be stored for a much longer time than many other crops.

Any worries that potatoes could cause leprosy were quickly dismissed in view of their useful attributes. Even in areas where cultivation of the potato was banned, peasants secretly grew potatoes because they quickly understood their value in a time when famine was striking various parts of Europe.

This was a difficult period for Europe. It's now known as the Little Ice Age, a period between the 16th and 19th centuries, when the overall temperature of the world dropped. This drop resulted in longer, colder and more severe winters. Springs and summers had a lot more rain and cooler nights, so many grain crops were destroyed.

Potatoes were much hardier than the grains commonly grown by European farmers and peasants. They could handle the lower temperatures and wetter summers.

And although potatoes were more labor intensive in the planting and harvesting periods, they yielded two to four times more calories per acre than grains. The improved food supply greatly reduced death by starvation among the peasants and increased the birth rate in Europe.

One Prussian ruler was so impressed with potatoes that he ordered all peasants to plant potatoes or else they would have their noses and ears cut off. As a result, potatoes became popular in Prussia. When Prussia was repeatedly invaded by France, Russia and Austria in the Seven Years' War starting in 1756, many of the peasants who previously would have died of starvation during these conflicts were able to survive because of their diet of potatoes.

France, Russia and Austria took note of the reason behind the Prussians' resilience and began to induce their peasants to grow potatoes.

A French doctor named Antoine-Augustin Parmentier was instrumental in promoting the potato in France. While serving as a pharmacist for the French army during the Seven Years' War, he was captured by the Prussians. He was imprisoned for three years in Prussia and fed a diet of mostly potatoes.

After his repatriation to France, Parmentier spent the rest of his life studying potatoes. His seminal work, *Examen Chymique des Pommes de Terres*, published in 1774, caught the attention of King Louis XVI and his wife, Marie Antoinette. They strongly supported the growing of potatoes, and Marie Antoinette once wore a headdress made of potato flowers at a royal ball.

One story relates that Parmentier got French peasants interested in the potato through a bit of a ruse. When he first received the king's permission to plant an acre of potatoes in the French countryside, he ensured it was thoroughly guarded during the day. At night, though, he left the land unattended.

Peasants in the area assumed that something guarded so heavily must be extremely valuable. Sneaking in at night, they stole many of the crops and planted them in their own plots. And thus the potato spread across France.

Even though this story can't be substantiated, potatoes became extremely popular in France. In less than half a century, French production rose from no potatoes at all to almost 3400 bushels in 1840.

The Russians had also seen the value of potatoes during the Seven Years' War. A serious failure in grain crops and famine in Russia and other Eastern European countries resulted in potatoes more quickly becoming a staple food for these countries.

The Potato Finds Its Way to England and Ireland

Not long after the Spanish introduced it to southern Europe, the potato came to England. Sir Francis Drake, the great

English privateer, found potatoes in the holds of the Spanish ships he had captured and brought the new plants back to England. The English climate was perfect for potatoes, and they spread throughout the country. Their impact on England and the rest of the world was felt much later.

During the Industrial Revolution in the mid-19th century, potatoes became a quick and easy way to feed the new urban-based workers for the new factories. Although the workers lived in small, squalid homes with barely a yard or no yard at all, they were able to grow many potatoes on tiny garden lots either near their homes or in wilderness areas near their workplaces. Frederick Engel, the German philosopher who wrote the *Communist Manifesto* with Karl Marx and who edited Marx's *Das Kapital*, considered the potato equal to iron for its "historically revolutionary role."

But the potato played an especially pivotal role in one country's history, where it would be part of a watershed moment that not only changed that country but also affected many other parts of the world.

When Spanish sailors and explorers brought potatoes home and tried to cultivate them themselves, they discovered that most of their country was too dry. Only a few isolated mountain areas—and the Basque region near the Atlantic coast—could successfully grow potatoes. With potatoes readily available, the fishermen of the Basque region were smart enough to realize that they made a good food to take along on their long trips to the Grand Banks (near what is now Newfoundland), where they caught most of their fish.

Once they had caught enough fish to fill their ships, it was routine for these Basque fishermen to stop in Ireland on their return trip home. They would go ashore in Ireland to dry their fish. Of course, they traded with the locals, and, sometime in the 14th or 15th century, potatoes came to Ireland. Their impact on that land is one of the most tragic and important in the story of the potato.

By the mid 1800s, potatoes were being cultivated on one-third of the land in Ireland. The idea that the Irish Famine of the mid-19th century was caused by potato blight destroying the crop is overly simplistic. The political and economic situation at the time also played a major role.

Following the defeat of the Irish by British troops under the command of Oliver Cromwell in the late 1700s, the English attempted to displace the mostly Catholic population and culture of Ireland. They did so by seizing land owned by the Irish and giving it to the English veterans who had won the war. This tactic didn't work, because the Irish culture was much too strong to be removed in such a way. And the English veterans were unable to profit from their new farms because they were using English-style crops and techniques. Ireland's environment was too damp, even by English standards, for their style of agriculture to succeed.

Therefore, many of these veterans sold their lands to a few wealthy land speculators. These absentee landlords then turned to cattle farming and meat production to turn a profit. They also hired cheaper Irish laborers to oversee their lands and their livestock. All the cattle raised in Ireland were slaughtered there as well. But almost all this beef was sold and shipped to markets in

England and other areas of Europe. Consequently, almost no one in Ireland, save for a few, had access to this meat.

In order for the Irish populace to survive, they began to grow potatoes, becoming completely dependent on their small crops to feed their families. Thus, when potato blight struck and spread across the island in 1845, almost all the potato crops in Ireland were destroyed, denying the typical Irish peasant their primary source of food.

Many cows were still being raised and slaughtered during the blight and famine, but even then, the absentee English landlords refused to allow any of the meat to be used to feed the people of Ireland. Most of it was still shipped off-island. That refusal, along with the potato blight, resulted in the catastrophic Irish Potato Famine that occurred approximately in the years between 1845 and 1850.

Within the first two years of the famine, over one million Irish perished as a result of hunger, typhus or any of a number of resulting diseases. Over one million more Irish fled their blighted lands, mostly to America and Canada.

The Irish Diaspora had significant effects on the lands where these new immigrants settled. These formerly rural Irish moved mostly to urban areas, such as New York City, Boston, Toronto, Montreal, Philadelphia and Baltimore. The result was that the Irish population in these cities grew dramatically, until they made up one-quarter of the population of the American cities and nearly one-half of Toronto's population. The new Irish became a major socio-economic and political force in several of these cities, and in many cases they still retain their strong roles and ties to those cities.

By the end of the 1850s, more than half of the people immigrating to the U.S. were Irish. And this form of mass emigration from Ireland continued for the next century and didn't truly drop until the 1960s.

The effect on Ireland was incredible. Before the Great Famine, the population of Ireland stood at 8.2 million. The present population is now 6.1 million, and at no time between now and then has the population returned to its pre-famine level.

The famine also further deepened the Irish bitterness toward the English. Many Irish nationalist groups were formed as a result of the famine and the role of the British in it.

Almost all the key historical moments in Irish history afterward—from the failed Easter Uprising of 1916 to the development of the Anglo-Irish treaty, from partition to the Troubles of the late 20th century—are indirectly a result of the Great Irish Famine.

There is no doubt that the famine in Ireland is the watershed moment in modern Irish history, affecting not just those who live in Ireland but all Irish people, wherever they now live.

As an added note about the famine, in 1847, a group of Choctaw Natives raised $710 and sent it to Ireland as a small token of relief. It wasn't much, but if one considers the circumstances, it was a poignant offer of help. Barely 16 years earlier, the Choctaw Nation had suffered through the Trail of Tears, a forced removal of more than 15,000 of them from their traditional lands in the American South. The Indian Removal Act of 1830 forced these Natives to march hundreds of miles to Oklahoma. Over 4000 of the 15,000 Choctaws removed from their traditional homes died during the trek, either from exposure, disease or starvation.

When news of the famine in Ireland spread throughout the world, the surviving Choctaws felt a sort of kinship with the Irish because of their suffering. So they gathered what they could and sent it over.

Spreading to the Rest of the World

Other parts of the world weren't immune to the charms of the potato. In Asia, potatoes first gained acceptance not as a food for the common people but as a delicacy among the Chinese imperial family. But as the population in China increased substantially in the years between 1735 and 1796, the need arose for a more substantial and hardier crop than grain. The potato filled that need quite easily. Potatoes also spread to nations such as India, the island of Java and the Philippines.

The potato also became part of already-established religious celebrations. The Jewish holiday of Hanukkah is an eight-day festival to celebrate the rededication of the Holy Temple around 200 BC. According to the Hanukkah legend, the people of Israel expelled the forces of Antiochus IV from their temple. But when they came to light the menorah (traditionally an oil lamp) for the rededication, they discovered that they had only enough oil for the flames of the menorah to burn for one day.

According to the Jewish book of the Talmud, the oil lasted for eight days, enough time for new oil to be created and sanctified by the priests. To commemorate the miracle, it is customary to celebrate Hanukkah with foods fried in oil. Bread was a choice for centuries. But in Eastern Europe, especially in the flourishing Jewish communities of Poland, Jews started using potatoes. Bread and grains were often difficult to come by. Potatoes, on the other hand, proved to be much hardier and easier to grow or obtain during times of famine and war. A flat potato pancake known as a *latke* was adopted as a food for the Hanukkah celebration. The tradition spread, and in many Jewish communities around the world, potato latkes are now an integral part of the Hanukkah celebration.

The Modern Potato

Nowadays, potatoes are enjoyed by a wide variety of peoples and cultures. They are grown in many countries and climates. China leads the way, with over 77 million tons grown annually. In all, over 347 million tons of potatoes are harvested every year around the globe, making it the fourth most popular food in the world.

One of the most common ways people eat potatoes is in chip form. From Canada to India, Japan to South Africa, potato chips are one of the most widely sold snack foods ever, creating a global market worth over $14 billion. Potato chips also come in a wide variety of flavors, including ketchup, cucumber, wasabi, Bolognese, horseradish, caviar and countless others. Name any food dish, spice or seasoning from anywhere in the world, and chances are there is a potato chip with that flavor being sold somewhere.

Not bad for a snack food that was created out of anger. The story goes that the potato chip was invented on August 24, 1853, at Saratoga Springs, New York. One night, a patron—said to be railroad magnate Cornelius Vanderbilt, one of the richest men in U.S. history—kept sending his fried potatoes back to the kitchen. The complaint? They were too thick, too soggy and not salty enough.

Agitated by this situation, resort chef George "Speck" Crum cut the potatoes wafer-thin. He then fried them crispy brown and covered them in salt. The customer loved them and soon the newly named "Saratoga Chips" became the toast of the town. Crum, self-described as the son of "a mullato jockey and an Indian maid," earned enough money from the sales of his chips to open his own restaurant.

These days it is estimated that the average North American eats six pounds of potato chips every year. But we wouldn't have the potato chip if it wasn't for the dish that preceded it: the fried potato. Or as most people commonly call it, the French fry.

Like its relative the potato chip, the French fry is one of the most popular food items on the planet. In North America, the average person consumes 30 pounds of French fries every year. And one-quarter of all potatoes produced in the U.S. are made into French fries.

In the UK, nearly one-half of all meals eaten outside of the home have some type of potato in them. And most of those potatoes are French fries, or "chips" as they call them there (and what Americans call "chips," the Brits call "crisps"). Despite the name, French fries are not believed to actually be French. Instead, it's the Belgians who have the strongest claim to this popular food.

It is said that in the late 15th century, residents of part of the Spanish Netherlands (later to become Belgium) invented fried potatoes out of necessity. In the long valley of the 500-mile Meuse River, peasants had a tradition of frying small fish to accompany their meals. But in winter, the river was frozen and the peasants had no fish to fry. So when the potato was introduced, they sliced them into fish shapes and fried those instead. The dish spread throughout the country, with vendors selling them on street corners. These types of fries are still sold everywhere in Belgium, and potato fries are the country's national snack.

Fried potatoes then made their way into France, and it was there, a few centuries later, that they caught the attention of Americans, who would take production of the French fry to incredible levels. U.S. soldiers fighting during World War II were introduced to fried potatoes while serving in France and Belgium. The Americans brought the idea back home, and presumably, French being spoken in both countries was a factor in calling them French fries.

But there is an earlier story about American exposure to French fries. From 1785 to 1789, Thomas Jefferson was the U.S. ambassador to France. While in Paris, he mingled with French society and sampled much of the fine culture, arts and cuisine that the city had to offer, including strips of potatoes fried in oil.

When he returned home, he served these "French potatoes" to his guests at dinner parties. When he became the third president of the United States, "potatoes served in the French manner" were on the menu during a White House dinner in 1802. Many food historians believe that Jefferson was the first U.S. adopter of this now-iconic American fast food.

A sample of modern potato dishes

But there's another story concerning Thomas Jefferson and a completely different influence of Native American culture. And its impact played a major role in the creation of the United States of America and was a key factor in the development of its supreme law: the Constitution.

Chapter Nine

The Great Law of Peace

The Five Nations

The people who would become the Five Nations had lived in the area of what is now the Finger Lakes region of upstate New York since the time the glaciers receded and left behind 11 thin lakes. The land was productive, full of fish and game. In time, the people learned how to grow maize, beans and squash. They called these three crops the "Three Sisters" and cultivated them strategically. The corn grew in tall stalks, the beans climbed up the stalks of corn and the leaves of the squash spread underneath both the corn and beans, which prevented the soil from drying and the sprouting of weeds. Using these techniques, a field would remain productive for decades. The people also gathered wild berries and fruits and tapped the abundant maple trees for syrup.

The inhabitants of this area lived in villages, in groups of 10 to 20 families, with each family living under the roof of an individual longhouse. The longhouses were normally arranged in a circle, and many villages were surrounded and protected by fortifications, such as walls made out of tree posts.

It is believed by many that the Iroquois nation was a key influence in the development of the Constitution of the United States.

The groups grew into the Five Nations, now known as the Seneca, Cayuga, Onondaga, Oneida and Mohawk. They battled other nations, such as the Algonquin to the east and the Huron to the north. They pushed the Algonquin even farther east and established a large territory in what is now the northeastern United States, with the Hudson River bordering to the east, the Delaware to the south and the St. Lawrence to the north, extending westward along the shore of Lake Ontario.

But when the Five Nations became the prominent culture in the area, something occurred. With a prosperous and growing population, they began to fight among themselves for goods, lands and people. Nations raided other nations. Villages raided other villages in other nations. Even villages from the same nation raided each other.

There were skirmishes and abductions, injury and death. Young warriors were glorified by their strength and action in battle, and for the spoils they brought back to their villages. But the traditions of the Five Nations stated that every violent incident, every attack, every kidnapping, every injury or death, had to be avenged with the same level of intensity, or more, by the family of the victim. Soon, the area became a fierce environment of brutality and violence, and many of the people lived in despair.

Deganawidah the Peacemaker

Sometime during this great despairing period, a great shaman roamed the land. Some said he was a member of the Five Nations, originally an Onondagan, but adopted by the Mohawk.

Others said he was an outsider. He had come from the north, it was claimed. He was a Huron. He had put his past behind him and paddled his way across great lands until he reached the Five Nations.

Still other people said he was the son of a virgin. One story has an old woman from the "Land of the Crooked Tongues" meeting the Great Spirit in a dream.

"Your daughter will bear a child," the Great Spirit told her. "And when this child has grown to manhood he will leave home and become the Peacemaker among the nations."

And this child was born, and he was strong and honest. But because he believed in peace and not war, many in his village did not respect him. So eventually there came a time when he had to leave. But instead of carving a canoe from a tree, he carved one out of white stone.

"The stone will float," he told his mother. "And by this the people will see that my words are true." Indeed, as he climbed into the stone canoe, it did float. And it moved forward without any paddling. It floated from his home village, through Lake Ontario and down into the land of 11 lakes, the lands of the Five Nations.

The child's name was Deganawidah. (It's interesting to note that some people allege that Deganawidah never existed, that he was only a name in a story. However, some of these same people believe in another man of great peace said to be of virgin birth, but who say that Deganawidah—a man also of great peace and a man of virgin birth—did not exist.)

As Deganawidah traveled through the lands of the Five Nations, he was not pleased by what he saw. But he had a solution. A solution of peace.

The first person to accept his message of peace was a woman named Jikohnsaseh. She lived in a small house along a trail that led into many of the Five Nations. And there she fed the hunters who passed by.

Even with Jikohnsaseh's acceptance, Deganawidah had trouble getting others interested in his ideas. Not because they weren't interested in peace, but because Deganawidah had trouble expressing himself. No matter what any of the stories say about Deganawidah, all agree that he had some type of severe speech impediment, probably a thick stutter. And that made it difficult to explain his law of peace to the warring nations.

Among the Onondaga lived a great warrior and orator. The Europeans came to know him as Hiawatha and managed to confuse him with the hero of the 1855 epic poem by Henry Wadsworth Longfellow. But the actions of Longfellow's romanticized "Indian"—who asked his people to welcome and accept the teachings of "the Priest of Prayer, the Pale-face" and "the Black Robe Chief"—are far removed from the actions of the great Onondagan orator. The true name of the renowned Onondagan was Ayenwatha.

Although Ayenwatha was a great warrior of his people, he had grown tired of the constant violence throughout the Five Nations. There had to be a better way to live, he realized. And when Deganawidah came and told him of his Great Law of Peace, Ayenwatha knew he had found that better way. He agreed to become Deganawidah's voice and would help spread the word of peace throughout the land.

But getting people to listen to the message remained difficult. The chiefs and their warriors were so caught up in the cycle of violence, glory and revenge that even talking of peace was considered an act of betrayal to the nation of whomever dared to speak of such a thing. So when Ayenwatha and Deganawidah approached Tadodaho, the most powerful chief in the Onondagan Nation, their talk of peace was met with violence.

Ayenwatha's three daughters were killed in the resulting conflict, and for a moment it seemed that he would abandon the plan for peace in order to avenge the death of his girls. But then he realized that if he did, some other parent would experience the same great grief that he had experienced at the death of his daughters. Thus, he decided to do whatever he could to prevent that kind of tragedy from happening again.

Spurned by the Onondagans, Ayenwatha and Deganawidah went among the other Five Nations to spread the law of peace. Of course, most were also caught up in the cycle of violence. Even those who were weary of war were skeptical that peace could be achieved.

When the two men met with the Mohawks, they didn't believe peace was possible. Intent on proving the power of his message, Deganawidah pointed to the top of a tall tree situated at the top of a high waterfall. "I will climb to the top of that water-fall and then the top of that tree," he told the Mohawks. "And then I ask you to cut that tree down. You say it is not possible for me to survive the fall from the tree and the waterfall, but I say it is possible that I will."

He then climbed to the top of the waterfall and then to the top of the tree. And although the Mohawks did not wish to cut the tree down, Deganawidah insisted. So they did. And the tree fell down into the waterfall and disappeared into the roaring river below. From their vantage point, they could see nothing and assumed that Deganawidah had perished—and along with him, his pleas and hopes for peace.

But when the Mohawks climbed down from the top of the waterfall, they found Deganawidah sitting by the bank of the river, stoking a newly made fire.

The Mohawks then believed that peace was possible. And they agreed to form an alliance with the other nations.

For the next several years, Deganawidah and Ayenwatha traveled throughout the Five Nations, going from village to village, giving the people a hope for peace. More and more villages agreed, and soon four nations—the Seneca, the Cayuga, the Oneida and the Mohawk—agreed to form an alliance. Only the Onondaga refused.

Again, the two peacemakers faced Tadodaho. They met him in a parley—a peaceful meeting designed to discuss various matters. Despite the agreements between the other four nations, Tadodaho was still caught up in the cycle of violence. He didn't believe a lasting peace between the peoples was possible.

Deganawidah then held a single arrow in front of Tadodaho.

"Take this arrow and break it," he said.

Tadodaho took the arrow and easily broke it in half.

Deganawidah took five arrows and tied them into a bundle. He held the bundle of arrows in front of Tadodaho.

"Take these arrows and break them," he said.

Tadodaho took the bundle of arrows. He was a great warrior. He was the most powerful shaman in the most powerful nation out of the five. But he could not break the bundle.

Somewhat defeated but still defiant, he gave the bundle of arrows back to Deganawidah.

"If you are so powerful," he demanded, "then you break the bundle of arrows."

Deganawidah shook his head and said:

The bundle of arrows is not meant to be broken. Bundled together, they are strong, unable to be broken. But alone, by itself, a single arrow is weaker and can be broken. The Five Nations are those arrows. If they band together, they will remain strong. But if they don't, they will be broken and fall into darkness.

Tadodaho didn't dismiss Deganawidah's argument as quickly as before. He went back to his village to think about it. Some days later, the sun was eclipsed by the moon, and the area of the Five Nations was plunged into darkness.

Tadodaho took this astronomical event as a sign of what would happen if he spurned the chance for peace among the Five Nations. He agreed to join the alliance.

And thus the Great Law of Peace (*Gayanashagowa*) was created. With that step, the Five Nations came together to form the *Haudenosaunee* (also known as the Iroquois League or Iroquois Confederacy), one of the earliest and most extensive constitutional federal democracies known in the history of humankind.

Dating the Haudenosaunee

Although there is no definitive proof of when the Haudenosaunee was created, many scholars believe it was founded sometime between 1090 and 1450 AD.

Skeptical archeologists, however, say there is no evidence to prove that the alliance could have been established before 1450. And some have even gone on to say that an alliance of Native Americans could not possibly have survived so long, especially given that Europeans at the time were constantly at war and that alliances between the nations and city states of Europe constantly shifted.

Let us digress for a moment. In a similar way, other scholars of this type have alleged that there was no way Native Americans could have discovered the concept of zero and other important mathematical concepts, and that they did not do so, because Europeans did not discover these concepts on their own. The concept of zero and many algebraic concepts came to Europe from other cultures, such as India and Arabia.

In the Mesoamerican Long Count Calendar, a dating system developed by the Maya of Mexico and Central America, the digit zero was used as a placeholder in its number system. The Maya used a numbering system based on 20. Maya culture is said to have developed in 250 AD, hitting its Classic period around 950 AD and continuing until the arrival of the Spanish after 1492. And during this time, zero was an integral part of the Maya culture and numbering systems.

Other cultures, such as the Chinese and the Indians, had also developed the concept of zero. In Europe, though, the concept of zero confused even mathematicians as recently as the time of the Renaissance. Further, the Catholic Church banned the use of 0 and other Hindu and Arabic numerals—the numbers 0 to 9—as dangerous ideas as late as the 14th century. Which is one reason why, when you count up from the year one BC, you go directly to the year one AD—because the developers of that calendar, the Europeans, didn't have the concept of zero or were confused by it or afraid of it.

As this little digression showed, it's completely unfair to say something along the lines of "they couldn't have done this by this time because we couldn't and didn't do it by this time," when many times the evidence shows that the opposite is true.

Recent studies into the Haudenosaunee seem to favor a date earlier than 1450 for the creation of the alliance.

One Seneca researcher, Paula Underwood, counted the number of generations in the oral record and determined the alliance was created around 1150 AD. Two other researchers from Toledo University in Ohio, Jerry Fields and Barbara Mann, came up with an ingenious plan.

Using the still-existing Condolence Cane, a long wooden cylinder on which the Five Nations recorded the names of council members of the Haudenosaunee from its inception to 1995, they determined the number of people who had led the alliance. The leader of the Five Nations since its formation has always been called the Tadodaho, after the Onondaga leader who finally agreed to sign the alliance. Once Fields and Mann had determined the number of Tadodahos, they then turned to European and American history. The gathered the names of over 300 other people who held lifetime appointments—such as popes, kings, queens, U.S. Supreme Court justices and others—over a few centuries.

Once they found an average, they applied it to the number of Tadodahos for the Five Nations and determined that, based on this comparison, the Haudenosaunee was likely formed sometime around the 12th century.

Wampum belts were used to represent treaties or alliances. The Wolf Treaty belt (top) represented the alliance of Mohawks with the French. The wolves symbolize the "Door Keepers" of the league. The coming of Tuscarora in 1713 was commemorated by an alliance belt (bottom).

They further determined that the only total solar eclipse that could have been observed in the land of the Five Nations during the period under consideration was on August 13, 1142. The next one occurred almost 500 years later, near 1600. And even the most ardent skeptics agree that the Haudenosaunee was created before this later date.

Based on this research, the Haudenosaunee appears to be the second oldest representative parliament in history still in existence, after only Iceland's, which was formed in 930 AD.

Many historians remain skeptical about this early start. One of their key arguments is that North American Natives relied on oral traditions to record their history. The doubters suggest that oral history cannot be trusted to be accurate as it relates to dates and times. But the Great Law of Peace was also recorded on belts of wampum, woven belts to commemorate treaties and historical events and for personal transactions such as engagements and marriages. Wampum belts were sacred objects used not just to commemorate these major events but also as a memory aid to oral storytellers. Some wampum belts for less significant events and transactions could be as small as two or three inches long. Wampum belts for important treaties could be over six feet in length and contain as many as 6000 beads.

Wampum belts for the Great Law of Peace, produced in the 18th century and based on the original belts or copies of the original belts, are located at the Onondaga Longhouse on the Six Nations Reserve in New York State (the Five Nations became the Six Nations around 1720, when the Tuscarora joined). These belts had been held by the United States Government for over 100 years. But the National Museum of the American Indian finally returned the belts to their rightful owners.

Many skeptical historians say wampum belts aren't reliable because they aren't actual writing like the writing that Europeans and other non-American nations used, and that they can be interpreted differently by different people.

But Mann and Fields argued that such thinking is "capricious, and most probably racial, of scholars to continue dismissing the [Iroquois] Keepers [oral historians] as incompetent witnesses on their own behalf" (as quoted from *Dating the Iroquois Confederacy* by Bruce E. Johansen). Because the skeptical historians use only documentary sources with dates on them, and because only non-Indians conveniently left such documents behind, the Native American perspective is screened out of history, the pair argues.

Dismissing Native historical records as invalid because they are not written in the style of a European written language, with "proper European dates," is demanding an inappropriate standard of proof regarding the Iroquois League's origins and other Native American historical events. Bruce E. Johansen explains:

When such writing is the only allowable proof,
dating the Iroquois League's origins earlier than the
first substantial European contact becomes impossible.
One must be satisfied with the European accounts
that maintain that the League was a functioning,
powerful political entity when the first Europeans
made contact with its members early in the 1500s.

For her part, Mann argues, "What I imply is that there is no 'proof' of the League's origins 'written' in a contemporary (i.e., mid-sixteenth century) European language." Emphasizing the point, she adds, "In fact, what written records exist point in exactly the opposite direction."

Representative Parliament and the Great Law of Peace

The Iroquois Confederacy is a truly representative parliament. The Great Law of Peace involved more than a simple alliance. It was a comprehensive arrangement creating a detailed government structure that allowed for the leaders to confidently run their nations, villages and clans while putting limits on their powers and providing personal liberty and autonomy to villages and individuals within the member nations. It was, and still is, a powerful constitutional document.

The Great Law contains 117 principles, some as basic as setting up the structure of the government or how a person should mark that they are absent from their house. For example, Section 107 states:

A certain sign shall be known to all the people of
the Five Nations which shall denote that the owner
or occupant of a house is absent. A stick or pole in

a slanting or leaning position shall indicate this and be the sign. Every person not entitled to enter the house by right of living within it upon seeing such a sign shall not approach the house either by day or by night but shall keep as far away as his business will permit.

Others outline rights and liberties that are still powerful and that many people around the world today do not enjoy. Section 99 states:

The rites and festivals of each nation shall remain undisturbed and shall continue as before because they were given by the people of old times as useful and necessary for the good of men.

It seems relatively generic, but in truth, it provides for people to practice whatever religion they choose.

There are others that are plainly stated, such as Section 93:

Whenever a specially important matter or a great emergency is presented before the Confederate Council and the nature of the matter affects the entire body of the Five Nations, threatening their utter ruin, then the Chiefs of the Confederacy must submit the matter to the decision of their people and the decision of the people shall affect the decision of the Confederate Council. This decision shall be a confirmation of the voice of the people.

Or Section 24:

The Chiefs of the Confederacy of the Five Nations shall be mentors of the people for all time. The thickness of their skin shall be seven spans—which is to say that they shall be proof against anger, offensive actions and criticism. Their hearts shall be full of peace and good will and their minds filled with a yearning for the welfare of the people of the Confederacy. With endless patience they shall carry out their duty and their firmness shall be tempered with a tenderness for their people. Neither anger nor fury shall find lodgment in their minds and all their words and actions shall be marked by calm deliberation.

Structurally, the Great Law of Peace established a council of 50 sachems (chiefs). Each sachem represented one of the clans of the Five Nations. The leader of the council was chosen by and among these 50 sachems, and he would be the Tadodaho, who was not only the leader of the council but also the keeper of the council fire. To this day, the council fire of the Haudenosaunee still burns.

All decisions made by the council had to be unanimous, making consensus and compromise important to the smooth running of the council. Although there were still skirmishes, battles and even war from time to time, the Great Law provided procedures and rules on how to deal with such things.

For example, if one clan from one nation went to war with another, it was swift and quick, at least compared to wars in other nations. The warriors did not kill the women and children of the other nation. They did not sack and burn their lands afterward. They were also responsible for any orphans and were required to adopt and raise the children of the conquered as their own, without distinction.

Although the Tadodaho was the supreme leader of the nations collectively, the internal operations of each nation, clan and village were the responsibility of the people who comprised it.

Jikohnsaseh and the Role of Women

Council members (sachems) could only be male. But each clan also had its own separate clan leaders, and clan leaders could only be female. Although the role of sachem was a hereditary position that traditionally went to a nephew of the previous leader, it was the responsibility of the clan leader to choose which nephew would become sachem. If she deemed no nephew was suitable, then she chose someone else. She also had the authority to remove the sachem from office if the clan found his actions displeasing. And important matters required all members of the nations to vote on them, not just the men.

Female clan leaders also elected someone to be their leader, a woman who would bear the title of Jikohnsaseh. Because the woman whom this title honors was the first person to accept the ideas behind the Great Law of Peace and put her substantial political weight behind it, the Iroquois considered her to be one of the co-founders of the Iroquois Confederacy.

Deganawidah told her:

> *Because you are the first to accept the Great Law, you shall be called, "Jikohnsaseh, Peace Queen, Mother of Nations." When the peace comes, you—the women of the tribes—will choose and remove the chiefs. Their titles will be both political and*

spiritual and will always belong to the women, called "Clan Mothers." Women know the hearts of men better than men. Women are the connection to the Earth. They create and have the responsibility for the future of the nation. Men will want to fight. Women will now say "yes" or "no" to war. Men, whose nature it is to be warriors, may not always see clearly the path of Peace; but a woman who knows that she must bury her loved ones, the children she has suckled, she would see and know if the fight would be worth its cost in life and death. Women know the true price of war and must encourage the chiefs to seek a peaceful resolution.

In this way, women had much political power throughout the nations. They also had a lot of personal power. Because the Great Law of Peace had strong principles about personal property, women could have their own possessions—such as their own animals, their own fields on which to grown corn, beans and squash, and their own homes. They could trade, sell or buy whatever they wanted without needing permission from their husbands, fathers or brothers.

If a woman wanted to divorce her husband, even have him cast out of the village or the clan because of bad behavior or abuse, she could. Or other women could do that for her, if she felt frightened or threatened.

When a man married, he moved into his wife's longhouse with her family. If the couple separated, the home, tools and fields stayed with the wife to supply a means to provide for the children. The children belonged to the lineage of the woman, so that every child would have a family to nurture her or him, even if the father left or died in battle. These customs ensured that the women of the tribes would always be treated with respect.

Such attitudes and rights for women were completely unthinkable for the Europe of the Middle Ages. Even as late as the mid-20th century, many women of European origin in parts of North America did not have such political and economic power. And there are still many parts of the world where that is the situation.

There were also no limits on personal movement or a member's status in Five Nations society. Individuals had the right to live the life they thought or felt was right for them, as long as they did not cause suffering or encroach on the rights of others. Sure, there were probably responsibilities related to survival—such as collecting food, chopping wood and building houses—plus the typical familial and societal pressures present in most human groups. But the people of the Five Nations owed fealty to no one—no monarch, no priest, no landowner, no class.

This type of societal system was quite attractive to many of the Europeans when they arrived.

Of course, a lot of these Europeans had to be rescued first.

Chapter Ten

Saving Jacques Cartier and New France

A Golden Age for Spain

The discovery of the New World by the Europeans, as noted, changed the balance of power. Because of all the riches brought back from its newly conquered lands, Spain became the richest country in Europe. And because the Spaniards had the most money, they were able to build the best and biggest ships and to fund and equip huge armies, as well as to provide their citizens with new goods, products and opportunities. More money also meant more funding for arts, culture and architecture. The discovery of the New World sparked what is known as Spain's Golden Age, a period of time from 1492 to the 17th century.

Some of Spain's greatest artists, composers and writers— El Greco, Diego Velázquez, Cervantes, Tomás de la Victoria, Francisco Guerrero, Lope de Vega and many, many others—came to prominence during this Golden Age. A good number of Spain's great architectural wonders—such as Madrid's Plaza Mayor, the Palace of Charles V, El Escorial, the Granada Cathedral and the Cathedral of Valladolid—were built during this time.

And all this richness and splendor was the result of Spain's new connection to the Americas.

Other Europeans were quick to notice the wealth and wonders that Spain had brought back from the Americas, however, and they were keen to get some of it for themselves.

A Commission from the King of France

King Francis of France wanted in on the action. Thus, in 1534 he commissioned Jacques Cartier to find a way to the Orient around or through the New World. And to also find lands unexplored by the Spanish that France could claim as her own. The commission read that Cartier was to "discover certain islands and lands where it is said that a great quantity of gold and other precious things are to be found."

This voyage to the Americas had not been Cartier's first. He had gone along on an earlier trip to North America with Giovanni da Verrazano, an Italian explorer who had been hired by France to explore the coastlines of North America. Cartier's participation in this earlier expedition put him in good stead to lead new French explorations.

On April 24, 1534, Cartier left France with two ships and 61 men under his command. Within 20 days, he made it across the Atlantic to the coast of Newfoundland. Not impressed by what he thought was a barren and lifeless land, he continued onward, charting the Gulf of St. Lawrence and the coastlines of what are now PEI, New Brunswick and the Gaspé Peninsula.

Jacques Cartier, during his first interview with the Indians at Hochelaga, now Montreal, in 1535. The Natives saved the Cartier expedition by giving them a treatment for scurvy.

On a number of occasions he did encounter Natives, but for the most part the meetings were brief. Although there was some trading, most of the Natives weren't overly friendly to Cartier's expedition.

Only when he reached an area of the Gaspé Peninsula were the Natives more open to contact. Near the Baie de Gaspé, the expedition spotted a group of Natives on the coast. When Cartier and some of his men rowed ashore, they were greeted warmly by Chief Donnacona, who headed a group of St. Lawrence Iroquoians living in the settlement of Stadacona. They exchanged gifts and agreed to a loose alliance, with the hope of more trade between the two peoples.

However, before returning to France, Cartier angered the Natives by planting a large cross on the coast. The cross held a fleur-de-lis shield and plaque that read "Long Live the King of France." Cartier also laid claim to all the lands in this region in the name of the king of France.

Although none of the Iroquois present could yet understand or read French, they were acutely aware of what Cartier was doing. Intent on expressing their disapproval, Donnacona and three of his sons rowed their canoe out to Cartier's ships. Using sign language, Donnacona ensured that Cartier was aware that these lands belonged to his people, not Cartier's.

Somehow Cartier lured the chief and his sons onto one of his ships. And then he took two of the sons hostage. Cartier told Donnacona that he needed to take back some Natives to France to prove that he had "discovered" a "new world" and promised to bring them home afterward. Because Donnacona was on Cartier's ship and surrounded by the explorer's men, he had no choice but to agree to the terms.

It is during this voyage back to France that Cartier came up with a name for the new land. He asked one of Donnacona's sons what they called the land they lived on. The son told him the people called the place they lived *kanata* (the Iroquois word for "village"). Applying the term to the entire area he claimed to have discovered, Cartier wrote the word "Canada" on his charts and maps as the name of the land.

Fortunately, Cartier did return a year later with Donnacona's sons. He also brought gifts from the king of France to appease the chief. But the Native leader was still reluctant to help Cartier further. And he discouraged Cartier from proceeding any farther up the St. Lawrence River, explaining that if they went too far and left their return too late in the season, they would get trapped in the ice.

But Cartier disregarded Donnacona's warning. He suspected that the Natives didn't want him to continue upstream because the land was filled with more riches and treasures. He also thought the Natives were trying to prevent him from finding a passage to the Pacific that would lead to the Orient. So he continued upriver and soon found a large island, which is now the Island of Montreal. He explored the area, even climbing to the top of Mont Royal. Meanwhile, a group of men he had left behind near Donnacona's village started building a small fort, an act that irked the Iroquois.

When Cartier began preparing to return home to France, he realized that Donnacona had been correct in his warning. Ice blocked the river. Getting back to the Donnacona's village and the site of the new fort was difficult enough. Cartier knew now that there was no way they would make it out to open sea and France. They would have to spend the winter.

The French hunkered down, hoping to survive the cold, dark months. Relations between them and the Natives were strained, but there was enough contact and trade between the two groups that Cartier and his men had sufficient supplies at their disposal to make it through winter.

Unexpected Complications

As the winter wore on, both sides were struck with disease. They developed serious lethargy, spots appeared on their skin that turned into open sores and their teeth fell out. This disease was not entirely new to either side, however. Europeans had suffered from scurvy since before the time of Christ. During the Crusades, scurvy killed thousands of soldiers. Portuguese explorer Vasco da Gama lost 117 of his 170 crew to scurvy during his great expedition around the Horn of Africa to India in 1599. During Magellan's circumnavigation of the globe in the years 1519–21, 208 of the 230 crewmembers died as a result of scurvy.

The Natives blamed the French and vice versa. Relations became even more strained, verging on downright hostile. The disease took its toll on Cartier and his men. By February, of the 110 men on this expedition, every single man had contracted the disease, and over 25 of them perished.

But then, during one of his infrequent contacts with Donnacona's village, Cartier noticed an unusual sight. One of the chief's sons, Domagaya, one of the men he had kidnapped and taken to France, was suffering from the same disease that the French had contracted. But when Cartier saw the youth again, instead of being in a further deteriorated condition like the French, Domagaya was the picture of perfect health. Cartier realized that the Natives had some type of cure for this disease.

He at first worried that if he revealed the extent of the disease to the Natives, they would attack. And because of his men's diseased state, they would all be killed. But Cartier also realized that if he and all his men died of scurvy, his expedition would be considered lost and a failure to France. If that happened, there was no assurance that the king would fund another expedition. France could turn its back on the New World.

So Cartier begged for assistance. Because of Cartier's inconsistent dealings, Donnacona was reluctant. But not wanting to make a permanent enemy of the French—he wasn't sure if the

French would send more men—he relented and allowed his son to help.

Domagaya took the needles from a white cedar tree and boiled them in water, making a tea. He offered the drink to Cartier. He refused, thinking that Domagaya meant to poison him and the rest of his men. Fortunately for Cartier and France, a few of his men weren't worried about poison. They were so sick they were willing to try anything. They had seen how horribly and slowly some of their counterparts had died, and they figured that death by poison, if that was indeed what was being offered, was a much better option. They accepted Domagaya's tea.

Almost immediately, the men's health improved. We now know that scurvy is caused by a significant deficiency in vitamin C. According to modern studies on the white cedar tree, tea made from its needles contains 15 milligrams of vitamin C for every ounce of liquid. It was the perfect solution, which the Natives had known about for centuries.

In eight days, the white cedar tree was almost stripped of its needles and all Cartier's men were cured. Cartier was so impressed with the cure that instead of thanking the Natives, he declared it a miracle and a gift from God. His appreciation to the Iroquois for saving his men and France's expedition would come in another way.

During the times when the Natives and Cartier were getting along, Chief Donnacona told Cartier about the Iroquois legend of the Kingdom of Saguenay. The legend stated that to the north lay a land of blond white men who were rich in gold and furs. Some historians now say the story was meant to be considered mythical, whereas others suggest that it was a ploy by Donnacona to confuse the French—if the French believed a great and rich kingdom existed farther north, they would go there instead of returning to the St. Lawrence. Some scholars have even asserted that this legend was about the blond, white-skinned, heavily fur-clad Norsemen who had settled in Newfoundland centuries earlier.

Cartier took this story literally, and by spring, he and his surviving men were ready to go home to France and spread the story of this rich kingdom. And to raise another expedition to discover and conquer it.

In order to keep good relations between his people and the French, Donnacona offered four young female members of his tribe to go along with Cartier so they could retell the legend to the king of France in person.

But Cartier didn't believe that a few female Natives would be suitable narrators of this story for the king. A more powerful voice was needed. So he kidnapped Chief Donnacona, two of his sons and three other Natives. He forced them to return to France with him. Cartier promised Donnacona that the king of France would present him with wonderful gifts and allow him to return.

He would not make good on those promises, however. Although Cartier did return to North America, he did not lead the third expedition. One of the king's closest advisors, Jean-François de La Rocque de Roberval, was the leader. Cartier would act only as navigator. Although the members of the third expedition constructed a much larger settlement, a lack of preparation, the environment and continued hostile reactions from Natives who had seen a chief stolen from them resulted in the abandonment of the settlement.

Despite Cartier's failings, his legacy is that he was the first European to penetrate North America by progressing along a major riverway. And his charting of the St. Lawrence River and the Gulf of St. Lawrence played a major role in further European exploration and settlement.

Samuel de Champlain followed in Cartier's footsteps in 1605, and he founded the first permanent settlement in New France, Port Royal. This venture and subsequent others gave the French a solid foothold in North America. They established a lucrative fur trade that attracted more French and other Europeans, and the enterprize resulted in the subsequent founding of the nation known as Canada.

As for the Natives who had given Cartier and his men a cure for scurvy and saved their expedition, their story is not so happy. Chief Donnacona, his two sons and the other four Natives were forced to remain in France and died within five years of their kidnapping.

To the south, the story of Natives coming to the rescue of newcomers was a bit different, but in many ways it was also very similar.

Chapter Eleven

Rescuing Jamestown

John Cabot

England's first contact with the "New World" probably didn't come via John Cabot, as most history books have noted. For a number of years, Portuguese and Spanish fishermen had made an annual trek to the Grand Banks, just east of Newfoundland, to draw from the huge bounty of fish the area provided. On their way home, these fishermen stopped along the western coastlines of Ireland and England in order to dry their fish on the beaches and to trade with locals. Noting the abundant fish catches of the Portuguese and Spaniards, many industrious English fishermen decided to follow them. A few did report seeing long coastlines to the west as they fished. Whether any went ashore or established relations with the locals is not known. Fishermen were known for catching a lot of fish but not for keeping historical records.

Officially though, John Cabot (known as Giovanni Caboto in his native Italy) discovered a new part of the New World sometime around 1497. Legend has it that when he finally made landfall on the far eastern coast of Canada, he called the place a "new found land," hence its name today. Because they were in direct competition with Spain, the English tried to paint Cabot as a great explorer and his "discovery" as being as significant as that of Columbus. But their efforts failed.

One reason for this failure is that by the time Cabot finally made it across to the "New World," Columbus had already made two trips and was readying for his third.

A second, compelling reason is that there is no evidence that Cabot actually landed in the Americas. Almost everything that is known today about Cabot's famed second voyage comes from four short letters, all written by people who were not even part of the expedition, a number of them working from second-, third- or even fourth-hand information. And the letters have contradictory information about where and when Cabot landed and what actually occurred during the voyage.

The most reliable letter claims that Cabot did land in Newfoundland but stayed within 100 yards of the coastline and hung around only long enough to plant a cross and a flag and claim the land in the name of the king of England, it seems. Then he left. He didn't explore, nor did he see any Natives.

Despite all these uncertainties and apparently limited achievements, Cabot and his crew were treated as heroes in England. He met the king and was declared a discoverer of the New World. He was given permission to attempt a third voyage. His five ships left Bristol at the beginning of May 1498. The entire expedition disappeared. Cabot and his ships are believed to have been lost at sea.

Unfortunately for the English, Cabot's fate and the lacka-daisical way in which English expeditions seem to have been conducted set the tone for many of England's subsequent expeditions to the Americas.

The English Try Again…and Again

For the next century, the English made 18 attempts at establishing some kind of settlement in the Americas. Some of them were attacked and destroyed by the Spanish, some were attacked by the local inhabitants, and most of them suffered from poor planning and preparation.

Unlike French, Spanish and Portuguese expeditions, which were government backed and funded in the manner of a 1960s U.S. lunar trip, English forays into the Americas had little government funding. Most of these expeditions and attempts to establish colonies were private ventures, backed by private money interested only in making a quick buck. Many of these funders were companies listed on the stock market, and shareholders expected expenses to be kept low while maximizing profit. Therefore, the expeditions were poorly supplied, poorly prepared and poorly crewed.

And whereas the other European countries had crews who were used to hardship—such as sailors, soldiers, peasants and others—the English sent mostly middle-class types. Sometimes they just grabbed people off the streets, young boys mostly, and press-ganged them into service. Some people sent on these voyages were prisoners, either sentenced to a period of overseas indentured slavery or offered a choice of death or a sentence of banishment.

The crews of these expeditions were unused to the severe hardship that the Americas would present, and most were ignorant of basic skills such as hunting, trapping, fishing and farming.

The colonies that survived past the first year generally failed to produce enough profit for the shareholders and were abandoned. Sometimes the colonists themselves were left behind, and no ships returned to resupply them or to take them back home. They were left at the mercy of starvation, disease, exposure or the local Natives. A few hardy colonists managed to survive this abandonment and, on a number of occasions, were adopted into local Native bands.

The Founding of Jamestown and Early Hardships

The Jamestown settlement was the perfect example of England's foray into North America. Bankrolled and backed by the Virginia Company of London, the Jamestown venture was designed to establish a permanent colony in America and produce profit from a wide variety of endeavors, including the cultivation of grapes for wine and olives for oil, the farming of various profitable crops, the mining of any metals they could find (preferably gold) and other possible income-producing industries, such as glassmaking and silk weaving.

But even though this venture was England's 18th attempt to establish a permanent and profitable settlement, the founders had learned little from the previous ventures of their countrymen. Again, the people coming to establish the colony were ignorant of many of the skills that were needed to ensure the success of the venture. A large number of the colonists were "gentlemen explorers"—second or third sons of noble and sometimes rich families who, because of their birth order, would not inherit any of their family's estate. Most had no real prospects of a career except in the army or in some other venture that was socially acceptable for the son of an English noble. So most of them, along with the others along for the ride, had no expertise for living in the wild, even though they were ordered to build a settlement in the wilderness. They had no background in farming, even though they were expected to cultivate crops such as olive trees or grape vines. And almost all had no experience with extremely hard labor, the type of labor required to build and sustain a new settlement in a completely foreign land.

In early December 1606, three ships—the *Susan Constant*, the *Godspeed* and the *Discovery*—left London with a crew of 39 sailors plus 104 men and boys who were expected to be colonists. The date of their departure was already a mistake. Crossing the Atlantic in the middle of winter can be a highly risky proposition, even today. As a result, to reach the coastline of Virginia, near the mouth of Chesapeake Bay, it took these three ships 144 days—a long voyage even in those times.

And out of 143 people who had set out from London, only 104 managed to survive the Atlantic crossing. The death rate once they made land became even worse; most of the settlers didn't survive the first year.

As per their orders, the expedition sailed farther inland to establish a settlement that would be protected from sea-based attack. At the time, the Dutch, the Spanish and the French were also establishing colonies, and although there was no declaration of war, each nation did not hesitate to attack the colony of another.

Farther up the river, which they named the James River to honor the king of England at the time, the colonists found an island that they thought would be perfect for their new settlement. It was sufficiently far inland so as not to invite a sea-based attack. And, being an island, it would also be less prone to attack by the local Natives. It was also uninhabited.

They named the island and the settlement after the king. The official title was "James, His Town," but it quickly became known as simply Jamestown. Even though the colonists had little experience in establishing a colony or with hard labor, they were quite industrious during their first weeks. Within a fortnight, they had cleared about an acre of land and built a rudimentary fort that featured several buildings for lodging and storage of goods, a glass-blowing furnace, surrounding walls and a church.

Things were starting to improve; the colonists were relatively established and were already producing some glass objects and items that could be sent back to England to be sold. They had also found what they believed to be a supply of gold and worked very hard to mine it and load it into the ships.

Their situation, however, started to turn. Even though the colonists were expected to live in this settlement for at least a year before being resupplied, they did not bring enough food to last the year. The colonists were expected to find their own, either through hunting, fishing or growing their own.

But because they had established their colony on an island, there was no large game to hunt. In a very short period, most of the small game on the island had been killed and eaten by the colonists.

They did attempt to plant crops, but they planted them too late in the growing season, so by the time winter came, there was little to harvest. And because the island was mostly marsh, finding arable land on which to plant crops was difficult. The marsh was also infested with mosquitoes, the right kind to spread malaria, a disease that killed many of the colonists.

And because the island was located in the tidal region of the James River, they had no access to fresh water. Although the colonists drank water from the river, it was brackish and led to many instances of saltwater poisoning as well as diseases, such as dysentery, and resulted in infections and fever. Many colonists died as a result.

The colonists were discovering for themselves that there was a reason the island was uninhabited, why no Natives lived on the island now called Jamestown. It was mostly useless for survival purposes.

The colonists were expected to trade with the local Natives, but relations were strained. It didn't help the colonists when they opened fire during their first meeting with the Natives, killing several warriors. In response, the Natives attacked the colony in the first month, killing a few of the colonists.

For the next several years, the colonists and the local Natives maintained a fractured relationship. Sometimes relations were peaceful, and there was trade. But mostly, the Natives didn't trust the English. Their first meeting with the newcomers had resulted in a number of deaths. And one of the leaders of the colony, Captain John Smith (yes, the one who claimed that Pocahontas saved his life) was a major thorn in the side of the Natives. Unlike most of the other colonists, Smith had experienced survival conditions during his years as a mercenary, pirate and soldier.

Captain John Smith is rescued by Pocahontas. Although this story has been told over and over again, and both Smith and Pocahontas existed, the events depicted here are believed to have been fabricated by Smith.

Smith did all he could to get food for the colonists, including trying to turn the various Native tribes against each other and executing raids to steal food from the Natives. At one point, Smith and the chief of the local Natives came to an agreement. The Natives would give the English a shipload of corn, and in return they would receive a grindstone, 50 swords, some guns, a cock and a hen, copper and beads and the use of some men to build an English-style house for the chief. Smith even sent four German colonists to start building the house, but he had no plans to honor the rest of the deal. Instead, he headed upriver with a small force of men, intent on surprising the Natives and stealing the corn.

But the Natives got word of the attack and lay in wait. Smith suspected the Natives would be waiting, so a standoff ensued. During negotiations, Smith attacked, and in the following melee he managed to grab the local chief and hold a knife against his throat. He threatened to kill him unless he and his remaining men were free to leave with all the corn. The Natives backed off and let him go.

What about the details of the Pocahontas story, in which a Native princess falls in love with Smith and throws her body against him to protect him from execution? Well, most scholars nowadays believe that story was fabricated by Smith. He had previously recounted a very similar story regarding his time as a mercenary in Turkey.

Another way the colonists riled the local people was by letting some of their livestock trample through the Natives' crops of corn, beans and tobacco or simply helping themselves to them. The thinking of the English was that because the crops weren't contained or held in by fences to keep out trespassers, they were free for the taking.

The colonists believed—as some historians still believe even today—that the Natives were savages, simple hunter-gatherer tribes who lived a subsistence existence and thus were unable and unwilling to share food with the civilized English. Never mind that these people lived in villages much larger than Jamestown and these villages had numerous longhouses, fortifications and storehouses. And that the lands around Jamestown were covered in fields of cultivated corn, beans and tobacco.

The Powhatan Confederacy

When the first Europeans arrived, the Natives living in the Jamestown area were by no means simple savages. They had evolved a highly sophisticated culture, a significant alliance of nations almost 20,000 strong, that stretched across what is now Virginia.

These Algonquin-speaking Natives were all part of the Powhatan Confederacy, an alliance of many nations who lived in this locality. As with the Iroquois Confederacy to the north, the Powhatan was a federal organization, in which there was a centralized government and leader, located in the town of Werowocomoco. At the same time, each nation or village in the alliance controlled their own local matters. And, as in the Iroquois Confederacy, there was a high level of personal liberty.

The leader of this alliance was named Wahunsenacawh, but the English called him Chief Powhatan. As a result, in many histories about the Jamestown settlement, the leader of the Native people is called Chief Powhatan, despite it not being his real name.

The Powhatan main center of Werowocomoco was long believed to be a Native village that was slightly bigger than others in the Powhatan Confederacy, but recent archeological digs have shown otherwise. It wasn't just a more sizeable village but a major regional center, said to be over 50 acres in area and to have been populated by a large number of people since the 13th century. Also on the site are two impressive D-shaped earthworks, ditches more than 200 feet in length. These ditches are said to indicate centuries-long settlement of the area. Archeologists also note that such earthworks were often integral to a ceremonial site or used to define a sacred space.

The Powhatans were also sophisticated farmers, as shown by the wide-ranging fields of corn, beans and tobacco throughout the alliance. It would be one of these crops that would save the English.

Although the Powhatan could have easily wiped the English from the land, it is widely believed that the reason they did not do so is because the Natives didn't consider these white men to be much of a threat, even though they were annoying. And although the Powhatans didn't truly like Captain Smith, they did have some respect for him as a warrior and as a protector of his people.

The Powhatans also didn't believe that the English would survive anyway, because within the first year of their arrival, only 39 of the original colonists were still alive.

Further Hardships for Jamestown

Within weeks of their arrival, the colonists did manage to send the *Susan Constant* back to England filled with what they thought was gold, the glass items they had made, plus some soap and wood products. But the gold was actually pyrite or "fool's gold," and therefore worthless. And the other goods did not yield enough to pay back the initial investment.

When the first resupply ships from England showed up at the colony in January 1608, they had both more supplies and additional settlers. But again there wasn't enough food to last, and even more colonists died of starvation, disease and exposure. By the time the second supply fleet arrived in fall, bearing still more new inhabitants, only 69 colonists were alive. The conditions were so challenging that, for almost the first decade of the Jamestown settlement, the average life expectancy of a colonist was just one year.

Despite the hardships and suffering at Jamestown, the corporate bosses were displeased and made even more demands. They expected the colonists to send back enough goods to pay back the cost of the return voyage of the ship, a lump of gold and a member of the lost Roanoke colony. This other colony had been established by Sir Walter Raleigh in 1585 and, after three years, had disappeared without a trace. Even to this day, no one truly knows what happened to the members of the lost colony.

The financiers also exhorted the settlers to plant grapevines, create silk cloth and dig for more gold. There were new laws against idleness, and if a colonist missed church three times in a row, for whatever reason, the penalty was death.

Even Captain John Smith was almost killed. While he was crossing a river, his gunpowder pouch exploded. He was injured and went back to England for medical treatment.

With Smith gone, the colony fell apart and deteriorated further. During 1609–10, the colony went from 214 men to fewer than 60. A hurricane caused the main supply ship to be shipwrecked on Bermuda. The survivors of the shipwreck managed, over the space of nine months, to build another ship out of the wreckage and make it to Jamestown. However, they had lost many of their supplies during the accident. Consequently, the colony had more people to feed, but no additional food.

Giving up, the surviving colonists gathered all they could and took two of the smaller ships and abandoned Jamestown. However, before they made it out to sea, they ran into a flotilla of three more supply ships. They were commanded by a strong leader, Governor Thomas West (later Lord Delaware), and this time the ships had brought enough provisions. They also brought a doctor. The new governor commanded the colonists to turn back, and Jamestown was once again inhabited.

John Rolfe's Idea and Pocahontas

One of the people who had survived the shipwreck on Bermuda, and who had hoped to make his fortune in Virginia, was a man named John Rolfe. His family had perished in Bermuda during the shipwreck, but while he was trapped on that island, he gathered up some tobacco seeds and took them to Jamestown, which he reached on May 14, 1610.

Unlike the rest of the colonists, who were still trying to grow olives and grapes, to weave silk and to search for and mine metals, Rolfe thought tobacco growing would be the better choice. But like many of his other countrymen, Rolfe had no experience in farming, especially in the unfamiliar crop of tobacco.

In many histories of Jamestown and the United States, it simply says that John Rolfe started growing tobacco, thereby saving the colony of Jamestown. But these histories miss an important detail: growing tobacco isn't easy. Rolfe didn't just plant his seeds and wait a few months for a tobacco crop to come out of the ground to be harvested and sent to England. It took him up to two years just to figure out how to grow tobacco and another two years to learn the curing process. None of the other colonists had any idea how to grow tobacco, and there were no texts available to teach Rolfe how to grow, harvest and cure tobacco.

The Powhatan Natives knew how to grow and cure tobacco, though, because they had been doing it for centuries.

Growing tobacco isn't like growing most other crops. It is a very delicate plant that needs much care and attention. The seeds first must be evenly scattered across the soil. And because they require a fair amount of light to germinate, they are not buried in the soil, as with many other crops. Also, they need adequate fertilizer and just the right level of moisture. Too little or too much, and the crop can be ruined.

Harvesting the tobacco leaves was labor intensive. The leaves had to be picked one at a time, handled gently, and then wrapped in bracken fronds so that they could be moved out of the fields. Then they were alternately cured inside sweat lodges and outside in the sun. If the sweat lodge was too hot or too moist, then the leaves weren't useable. If there wasn't enough sunshine, or if the leaves were left outside too late in the day, the crop could be ruined. In autumn, the leaves were laid outside every morning to absorb dew.

In order to get seeds for the next year, the seedpods were tied in small bunches and hung inside all winter, where they were blackened by the smoke of the indoor fires. After winter, these bunches were taken down and crushed, and the seeds were evenly scattered across the fields for the next crop. All these tasks required a lot of work and attention. The growers had to be delicate in their actions and watchful of both the weather and the indoor temperature and humidity, or a year's work could be ruined in just a few hours.

John Rolfe watched the Natives harvest and cure their tobacco, and he painstakingly worked to imitate them. He also had some inside help.

Not long after Rolfe arrived in Jamestown, Pocahontas, who was the daughter of Chief Powhatan, was captured by the colonists. They had intended to hold her ransom for food, weapons and other colonists who had been previously captured by the Powhatan. And although the Natives returned the captured colonists to Jamestown, the English didn't return Pocahontas. They kept her imprisoned for over a year.

The English are said to have treated her well, teaching her English and persuading her to become a Christian. One of the people she met while in captivity was John Rolfe. He had lost his first wife and infant child during the Bermuda shipwreck, and although he was a serious and pious man, he was immediately smitten by the younger female Native. He claimed he was,

> ...motivated not by the unbridled desire of carnal affection, but for the good of this plantation, for the honor of our country, for the Glory of God, for my own salvation...namely Pocahontas, to whom my hearty and best thoughts are, and have been a long time so entangled, and enthralled in so intricate a labyrinth that I was even a-wearied to unwind myself thereout.

Rolfe asked the governor if he could wed her. Permission was granted, and they married in 1614. By this time, Rolfe had been able to grow a pretty good crop of tobacco, but he had yet to perfect the curing process. Pocahontas, who had learned these techniques from her people, passed them on to her new husband. Chief Powhatan also gave the newlyweds a large plot of land on which Rolfe could grow even more tobacco. Relations between the English and the Powhatan were cordial during these times. The Powhatan helped teach Rolfe and others more tips and techniques to grow tobacco and other crops, such as corn.

Two years later, Rolfe had enough tobacco for a commercial shipment back to England. He went along with the shipment, also taking his wife, now Rebecca Rolfe. The tobacco was a great financial success, and Rolfe returned to Virginia a rich man. Over the years, the shipments of tobacco increased.

In 1618, Jamestown shipped 20,000 pounds of tobacco. In 1622, it was 60,000 pounds. Within another five years, it was 500,000 pounds, and by 1630, more than 1.5 million pounds of tobacco were shipped.

"The discovery that tobacco could be successfully grown and profitably sold was the most momentous single fact in the first century of settlement on the Chesapeake Bay," Rolfe later wrote. "Tobacco had guaranteed that the Jamestown experiment would not fail."

Unfortunately, Pocahontas never returned to her homeland. After several months in England, she contracted a disease, either tuberculosis or smallpox, and died on March 21, 1617.

Upon hearing of her death, Chief Powhatan abdicated from his position and moved farther inland. His brother Opitchapam took his place as leader, but his younger half-brother Opechancanough was actually in charge.

Because of the phenomenal growth in the tobacco trade, thousands of English moved to America. The population of Europeans exploded. When the Jamestown colony was established in 1607, the number of English in the Americas was less than 1000. Within 50 years, there was at least 50,000. By the turn of the next century, there were almost 300,000. The English established colonies all along the Eastern Seaboard, from Maine to the Carolinas, pushing out the Natives.

The Powhatan Confederacy fell apart, destroyed by a combination of disease and destruction at the hands of British military forces. At the time of first contact with the English, the Powhatan numbered more than 30 tribes, with a population of over 15,000 members. They lived in over 200 villages in a territory exceeding 8000 square miles in size. By 1705, the descendants of the Powhatan numbered only 150 people who lived in about eight villages.

The English foothold on the Americas was permanent, and their empire spread, surpassing that of Spain. In time, the colonies of England would number 13. Those 13 colonies later became the original United States.

And much of the success of the English was possible because a woman named Pocahontas and other Natives of Virginia had passed on the secrets of tobacco to the English and helped rescue the Jamestown settlement.

Chapter Twelve

Tobacco

Native American Use of Tobacco

On October 12, 1492, Christopher Columbus arrived with his three ships, *La Niña*, *La Pinta* and *Santa María*, and "discovered" the New World. He first landed on the island of Guadeloupe and was greeted by a group of Natives. The Natives happily greeted Columbus and his men and, in recognition of the event, offered gifts of jewelry, beads and some leaves.

Although they were unsure what to do with the leaves, Columbus and his men accepted the gifts graciously. He knew he could easily subdue these people, but he thought he had arrived off the coast of Asia and that these people were subjects of the great Khan, the leader of Imperial China. Therefore, although he knew he had the superior fighting force currently in the area, he didn't want to offend anyone lest more powerful reinforcements be summoned.

A label for Pride of Columbus tobacco. It is interesting to note that Columbus and his men dumped the original gift of tobacco overboard.

After spending some time on the island, the men boarded their three ships and left. When they were out of sight of the Natives, they tossed the leaves overboard. Little did they know that this would be the first European contact with a plant that within a few centuries would reach into every single corner of the planet and affect every single culture in the world. Out of all the "gifts" given to the world by the Americas, tobacco was one of the most powerful.

Nobody really knows when the people of America started using tobacco. But by the time Columbus and the rest of the Europeans arrived in the Americas, tobacco was one of the most widely used items on these continents and on the offshore islands of the Caribbean.

Unlike many of the other crops used by North American Natives, tobacco wasn't one of sustenance. It was one of the items with the most diverse uses of anything on the entire continent. Tobacoo was smoked, sniffed, drunk, chewed and spit out, chewed and swallowed, smeared over the skin and hair, dripped into eyes, the leaves stuffed into body orifices, the smoke blown into faces, over bodies and sexual organs and delivered as an enema. It was also used as an aphrodisiac, a relaxant, a stimulant, an appetite suppressant, a painkiller, a remedy for snake bites and other wounds, a cure for fever, the common cold and the flu, a treatment for cancer and a social pastime. It was blown over women prior to sexual relations to ensure fertility. The leaves were waved over warriors prior to battle to ensure victory over their enemies and glory in battle.

Some types of tobacco the Natives used could cause hallucinations if smoked in high doses, and it became a key element for inducing spiritual journeys. Shamans of all nations used tobacco in vision quests or to reach a heightened state of being. In some tribes, shamans used tobacco (along with other hallucinogens) to achieve a near-death state. They entered this state in order to reach a higher spiritual level, to fight off evil spirits threatening their communities or to return with insights about how to treat a particular disease. Apprentice shamans went through rigorous training that involved repeated exposure to greater amounts of tobacco.

Unlike in recent times, during which most people who used tobacco did so by smoking it, the first—and for a long time the most common—method of consuming tobacco in pre-Columbian times was to chew it. Many societies eventually developed the concept of smoking tobacco, however. Some had elaborately designed pipes similar to the size of pipes today, and others built pipes so massive they had to be supported by Y-shaped branches about the same height of an average man.

But for an average Native American, chewing tobacco was logistically easier. Instead of stopping work—hunting in the woods, gathering berries or working in the corn fields—to fill up a pipe, create a spark with which to light it and smoke the tobacco, it was simpler to reach into a pouch and pop a pinch of weed into the mouth.

Tobacco was used by almost every single Native nation in the Americas, save for possibly the Inuit. It was so popular that many people always carried individual pouches of tobacco and used it every day, not only for personal use but also as currency.

Tobacco was so ubiquitous in the Americas that it is almost impossible to determine where and when it was first used and by whom.

There are over 60 species of tobacco plants, all members of the *Nicotiana* genus of plants and mostly native only to the Americas. The most common species were *Nicotiana tabacum* and *Nicotiana rustica*. Given that most Native American nations were extremely well versed in the use of herbs and that tobacco grew wild throughout many parts of the Americas, it's very possible that many nations discovered tobacco independently of each other.

In its early use by Native Americans, tobacco was probably just one herb among many. But as its uses multiplied—and also because it's highly addictive—tobacco became one of the most prominent and widely utilized plants in the Americas.

Even though no one has truly determined which Native group was the first to gather tobacco leaves, plant geneticists have surmised that the actual cultivation of tobacco, the moment people started growing tobacco as an agricultural product rather than collecting it from the wild, occurred around 5000 to 7000 years ago. Natives in the Andes mountains in Peru or Ecuador are said to be the first people who figured out how to grow their own tobacco. And once they worked out all the details, the knowledge quickly spread north until a larger number of Native nations were growing their own plants. They were also employing hybridization techniques to create strains of tobacco that would better thrive in the local climate. Some growers even created different strains of tobacco for more personal reasons, such as a preferred taste or the scent of the smoke.

Tobacco wasn't restricted in its use. Both men and women used tobacco on a regular basis. In some societies, even children as young as five years old consumed tobacco.

But once people started smoking tobacco—again, no one really knows who began this method of consumption, or where and why—Native Americans discovered a completely new means of consumption not previously seen in any part of the world.

"That lungs had a dual function—could be used for stimulation in addition to respiration—is one of the America continent's most significant contribution to civilization," wrote Iain Gately in his book, *Tobacco: A Cultural History of How an Exotic Plant Seduced Civilization*.

> *Human lungs have a giant area of absorbent tissue, every inch of which is serviced by at least a thousand thread-like blood vessels, which carry oxygen, poisons and inspiration from the heart to the brain. Their osmotic capacity is over fifty times that of the human palate or the colon. Smoking is the quickest way to the blood stream short of a hypodermic needle.*

Soon, smoking became one of the most popular methods of consuming tobacco. At first, it had personal and practical applications. Smoking tobacco to many was more pleasing than chewing the leaves, while at the same time increasing the effects of the plant. The smoke also became something of an insect repellent. Some societies blew tobacco smoke over corn fields and fruit orchards to control insect pests and as a blessing for a good crop. Some South American societies applied tobacco juice to their skin to kill lice, fleas and other skin parasites.

Within a few centuries, smoking tobacco moved from being a more personal habit into a social and spiritual practice, deeply tied to the culture of many Native American societies.

The smoking of tobacco was used by shamans and in spiritual rituals, such as sweat lodges, or prior to major celebrations. Sharing a smoke of tobacco was also a means for different tribes to connect with each other before, during and after treaty or trade negotiations.

In many localities, smoking societies were formed in which significant members of the nation met and smoked together in social, political or meditative sessions. At first, people just rolled tobacco leaves into tight cigar shapes and smoked those. Over time, however, the use of pipes became more prevalent.

In the Hopewell tradition of the Mississippi Basin of what is now the American Midwest, smoking tobacco in pipes was an important part of the social and spiritual aspects of their culture. The men of the Hopewell designed elaborate pipes out of stone and even copper. Some of these pipes are considered to be among the greatest pieces of art of pre-Columbian times. During the height of the Hopewell tradition, from 1500 BC to 300 AD, tobacco pipes were treasured possessions. A man's pipe was so important in the Hopewell tradition that, when he died, his personal pipe was buried with him.

Several societies imbued the importance of tobacco in so many of their ceremonies and rituals that they could barely function without it. Tobacco was one of the most important commodities in this entire section of the world.

"Isolated from the rest of their species for almost 18,000 years, the peoples of the Americans had matched or exceeded their overseas counterparts against many measures of cultural achievements," wrote Iain Gately in his book.

> *They had alphabets, pyramids and calendars. Their botanical knowledge and agricultural skills provided them with the resources to feed the great cities they established. The modern world is awash with daily reminders of these peoples' ingenuity, discoveries and art. And their most popular gift to the rest of humanity* [tobacco] *has since become its most common habit.*

European Smokers

When they arrived in the Americas, the Europeans couldn't help but notice all the people smoking. No matter where they landed or what areas they explored, the Europeans saw these new people in a strange land rolling leaves or pushing them into a pipe and putting the pipe into their mouths and then setting it on fire and breathing in the smoke.

"What did Europeans make of smoking? They had no precedents for the act," wrote Gately. "No one smoked anything in Europe. They burned things to produce sweet smells, to sniff but not to inhale. Smoke was for dispersal, not consumption. Without domestic precedents, the Europeans even lacked the vocabulary to describe smoking."

For most Europeans, the first time they saw someone smoke, they were incredulous at the sight. And they became more incredulous when they saw that almost everyone in the Americas had the habit.

Wrote bishop and historian Bartolomé de las Casas:

[M]*en with half-burned wood in their hands and certain herbs to take their smokes, which are some dry herbs put in a certain leaf, also dry, like those the boys make on the day of the Passover of the Holy Ghost; and having lighted one part of it, by the other they suck, absorb, or receive that smoke inside with the breath, by which they become benumbed and almost drunk, and so it is said they do not feel fatigue. These, muskets as we will call them, they call tabacos. I knew Spaniards on this island of Española who were accustomed to take it, and being reprimanded for it, by telling them it was a vice, they replied they were unable to cease using it. I do not know what relish or benefit they found in it.*

Many of the early Spanish leaders in the Americas found the use of tobacco to be offensive and even the work of the devil. One of the first governors of New Spain, Gonzalo Fernández de Oviedo y Valdés (in regard to the Caquetio of northern Venezuela) had this to say about the people and tobacco use:

They venerate and dread the devil very much, and the boratios [shamans] say they can see him and have seen him many times.... These boratios are their priests and in every important town there is a boratio to whom everyone goes to ask what is going to happen, whether it will rain, or whether the year will be dry or abundant, or whether they should go to war

*against their enemies or refrain from doing so,
or whether the Christians are well-disposed or will
kill them, or finally, they ask all they wish to know.
And the boratio says he will reply, after having
a consultation with the devil. And in order to have
the consultation he shuts himself into a cabin alone,
and there he makes use of some* [things] *which they
call tabacos, smoked with such herbs as deprive them
of sense; and one day, or two or three, passes and still
the boratio is shut up and does not come out. And as
soon as he comes out he says this is what the devil
tells him, answering the questions which have been
asked, according to the desires of those whom he
wishes to satisfy.*

Despite the hard line from the political and religious leaders against tobacco, its use became very popular among the Spanish hoi polloi in the Americas, as well as among sailors and average soldiers.

Indeed, the first European smokers were Rodrigo de Jerez and Luis de Torres, both crewmen on Columbus' first voyage. When the expedition made its second landfall, in what is now Cuba, Columbus ordered the two men to explore deeper inland to search for gold or possibly representatives of the Emperor of China. As they did in the first landfall on San Salvador, the two men were met by Natives who celebrated their arrival with a great feast and an offering of gifts, including another bunch of unusual leaves.

This time, though, Jerez and Torres had noticed that the Natives rolled the leaves tightly, lit one end and put the other end in their mouths to inhale the smoke.

They also saw some others use pipes to smoke the leaves. When the two crewmen returned to Columbus after four days in the jungle, they brought back the leaves and demonstrated how they were used.

When Columbus departed a few months later, Torres was left behind with a group of 38 other men, to build Spain's first settlement in the New World. However, he and the other members of the group were all dead by the time Columbus returned a year later. They were killed because many of the Spaniards abducted Native women. These acts prompted the local Natives to attack the settlement to rescue their women. The more religious members of the settlement were not only offended by these actions but also worried that the Natives would become even more angry if the abductions continued. A combination of Native reprisals for the abductions and violent Spanish in-fighting wiped out the settlement.

Jerez, meanwhile, had returned to Spain with Columbus, but even though he escaped death in Cuba, his fate back in Spain wasn't entirely pleasant. By the time his ship had left the Americas, Jerez was already hooked on tobacco and smoked it any chance he had. He introduced the leaf to his hometown of Ayamonte, but the sight of smoke encircling his head while he consumed the tobacco frightened his family and his neighbors. Their fear became so great that Jerez was later arrested and imprisoned by the Spanish Inquisition for smoking in public. Historical records are sketchy as to his sentence, but reports of his punishment range from three to seven years in an Inquisition dungeon. Ironically, by the time Europe's first smoker was released from incarceration, tobacco had become popular in Spain.

As noted, despite serious reservations by the Church and political leaders, tobacco's popularity increased among average Spanish sailors and conquistadors who, like many of the Natives, smoked it in pipes or as rolled leaves. Even the members of the lower clergy began using tobacco, but as snuff—a fine powder of tobacco leaves sniffed into the nostrils. Soon the two early major powers in the Americas, Spain and Portugal, began sending more and more tobacco back with their ships. Its presence wasn't as significant as the gold and silver these two countries were extracting from the Americas. However, it was getting some attention, especially from the king and queen, as well as the noble members of their court, who started growing tobacco in their gardens, first as an ornamental plant, and then to be ground into snuff.

In 1559, the French sent Jean Nicot to Lisbon, Portugal, as an ambassador to help arrange the marriage between the son of the Portuguese king and the daughter of the French king. Like many others Europeans, the French were quite envious of the success of the Spanish and the Portuguese in the Americas, and they continually looked for ways to share in the bounty. During his time away from marriage negotiations, Nicot begged for some tobacco cuttings from a Portuguese courtier.

Nicot was also an amateur botanist, and he had heard rumors of the healing properties of tobacco and decided to test them out. He found a man suffering from a cancerous tumor and gave him ointment made from tobacco to rub on his tumor.

Although there is no historical confirmation that the tobacco had cured the cancer, Nicot reported back to France that he had cured the man. He also sent seeds to the queen of France, the famed Catherine de Médicis. He advised her and the other members of the court that not only could a tobacco ointment be used to cure wounds and tumors, but its many benefits would also prevail if it was taken as snuff.

In a very short time, Catherine de Médicis was a regular snuff user, and so were the members of her court. Snuff became all the rage in France.

The Pope also became aware of Nicot's findings and reports and ordered tobacco seeds to be sent to the Vatican in Rome for further study. From the Vatican, tobacco spread, via members of the clergy, into the rest of Italy and into the Balkans. Nicot became known as the first major supporter of the use of tobacco for medicinal purposes. To honor his contribution, botanists would name the genus of tobacco plants *Nicotiana*.

In 1565, a Spanish doctor by the name of Nicolás Monardes published a pamphlet called the *Joyful News of our Newe Founde Worlde*. In it, he enthusiastically extolled the medicinal virtues of the tobacco plant and refuted accusations that tobacco was the herb of the devil. Monardes said tobacco was pretty much the cure for almost every human ailment from diseases of the internal organs to bad breath, and he recommended it for everything from kidney stones to helping heal wounds from a wide variety of sources, including poison arrows.

The *Joyful News* was translated into the major European languages—Latin, English, French and Italian—and prompted a continent-wide enthusiasm for tobacco, but mostly for medicinal purposes.

Tobacco Spreads to Asia and the Middle East

When Portuguese explorer Vasco da Gama headed south from Lisbon and circumnavigated Africa in 1497–99, to be followed in 1519–22 by the circumnavigation of the earth by Ferdinand Magellan's expedition, it opened the way for the Portuguese to establish trade routes and stations in places such as East Africa, India and Macau.

From these locations, via Arab traders, tobacco spread into the Middle East. The mostly Muslim countries quickly determined that because tobacco was not mentioned in any form in the Koran, it was not forbidden by the Koran. As a result, tobacco quickly spread through the Middle East.

But smoking the weed rolled up or in a pipe became a concern to some in the court of Akbar, the leader of the Mughal Empire in the northwestern part of India. They worried that breathing the smoke so directly from the leaves was a bit unclean. As a solution, the court physician, Hakim Abul Fateh Gilani, originally from Persia (Iran) came up with a novel idea. He thought the smoke would be purified if it passed through water, so he created a pipe that did just that—a device that was later called a hookah (also known as a narghile or sheesha).

Smoking through a hookah became popular with the Indian upper class and then spread to many countries in the Islamic sphere of influence. Over time, smoking tobacco in this manner became extremely popular, and it remains a significant social and cultural pastime in certain countries.

In Persia, during the 17th and 18th centuries (and in later centuries as well), a good number of people spent more money on an elaborately designed hookah, or *galyān* as it is called there, than they would on things like food or shelter. During his reign, Shah Abbās II (1642–66) had his own private *galyān* servant. And one of the shah's ambassadors to France even had a military officer whose job it was to hold the *galyān* so he could smoke while his carriage was in motion.

In many Middle Eastern and Arabic-influenced countries today, there are more café-style establishments where you can smoke tobacco in a hookah than places to buy a cup of coffee.

Surprisingly, the hookah's connection with tobacco is so entwined in many of these countries that for centuries it was commonly and reverently believed that tobacco originated from the same place the hookah did, from the East, specifically India. Even now, some people still have that belief.

In 1542, Portuguese sailors also took tobacco to Japan. According to some stories, a Portuguese ship carrying tobacco and seeds shipwrecked on an island owned by Japan, and through the incident, tobacco was brought to the attention of the Japanese emperor and his court. It wasn't long before the weed took hold in Japan as well. Samurai formed smoking clubs and commissioned artisans to create beautifully designed pipes, made mostly of silver. A samurai carried his pipe at all times, tucked into his kimono right next to his sword.

But the imperial love affair with tobacco eventually faded in Japan. From 1609 to 1616, it was banned four times, the most serious punishment being a combination of a fine, imprisonment and the confiscation of the guilty party's possessions and property.

Despite these attempts at prohibition, many people still smoked. In his book *Tobacco: A Cultural History of How an Exotic Plant Seduced Civilization*, Iain Gately notes that the bans were only cosmetic, and he relates a story in which the shogun's own body-guards openly smoked tobacco in front of him, even with the bans in place. And because they were ignoring an imperial edict, their punishment could have been decapitation. In 1625, all bans on tobacco were lifted in Japan, and soon the Japanese began offering pipes as gifts to guests.

It was also likely the Portuguese who introduced tobacco to the Chinese through their trading port in Macau. "Inquiring for the beginnings of tobacco smoking, we find that it is connected with the subjugation of the Yunan province," wrote Chang Chieh-Pin, a physician with the emperor's army.

> *When our forces entered this malaria-infested region, almost everyone was infected by this disease with the exception of a single battalion. To the question why they had kept well, these men replied that they all indulged in tobacco. For this reason it was diffused into all parts of the country. Everyone in the south-west, old and young without exception is at present smoking by day and night.*

By the 17th century, tobacco was present throughout Chinese society. But in 1640, the last Ming emperor placed a ban on smoking tobacco, and the penalty for breaking the ban was death. In response, the Chinese quickly turned to snuff, but the ban on smoking didn't last long. Within five years of the ban, the Ming Dynasty was over, overthrown by Manchu warriors from the north. The Manchus already had a love of tobacco, so when they took power, they lifted the ban and encouraged cultivation.

Scarcity and Bans in England

For Britain, tobacco is credited with saving the empire while at the same time playing a role in bringing down a king.

Sir Francis Drake and Sir Walter Raleigh get the credit for bringing tobacco from the Americas to England. But unlike their cousins across the Channel, the English couldn't care less if smoking tobacco was good for them. They just liked to smoke and sniff it and, like the Japanese, formed their own smoking clubs. The problem with the English and tobacco was two-fold.

First, when it was introduced in England, the English did not have their own supply. They had to rely on trade with foreigners, smuggling it or stealing it, which they usually did. English privateers regularly intercepted Spanish ships from the New World carrying riches such as gold, silver or tobacco. Because tobacco was so popular in England, by the early 17th century, the country was the largest tobacco market in Europe. At the same time, the new weed was scarce, so the tobacco in these captured ships was worth more than the gold and silver. In London, tobacco sold at four quid for one pound of tobacco. And that was only the wholesale price off the ship. In today's prices, that would be 700 GBP (USD$1120) for one pound of tobacco.

Sir Walter Raleigh's answer to the supply problem was to plant tobacco on his Irish estate, and others followed. Even so, the demand for tobacco kept increasing. Raleigh knew that the Americas were the perfect place for tobacco because he had seen so many Natives growing their own. So the idea was formed to send people over to the Americas and establish settlements, where they could get many riches, including tobacco. But most of these settlements failed, and, as noted earlier in this book, it was only when John Rolfe arrived in Jamestown, married Pocahontas and learned how to cultivate and cure tobacco that such a settlement did succeed.

By the time Rolfe got his first crop over to England, there were over 7000 shops in London selling tobacco.

Thanks to the Natives who helped Rolfe, the English had a regular supply of tobacco plus a thriving and permanent settlement in the New World. The success of Rolfe and Jamestown soon led to even more settlements, which resulted in England once again controlling one of the most powerful empires on earth.

But even with a steady and growing supply of tobacco that helped establish a foothold in the Americas and fuel the expansion of the British Empire, the supreme leader of it all, King James I, detested the weed, which is the second difficulty the English faced in regard to tobacco.

A serious, strict and highly religious ruler, James I was known for strong edicts against sin and vice, and for overseeing the torture and burning of women he thought were witches.

In 1604, James wrote his own treatise against tobacco, "A Counterblaste Against Tobacco." In it he stated:

> *Have you not reason then to bee ashamed, and to forbeare this filthie noveltie, so basely grounded, so foolishly received and so grossely mistaken in the right use thereof? In your abuse thereof sinning*

against God, harming your selves both in persons and goods, and raking also thereby the markes and notes of vanitie upon you: by the custome thereof making your selves to be wondered at by all forraine civil Nations, and by all strangers that come among you, to be scorned and contemned. A custome loathsome to the eye, hatefull to the Nose, harmefull to the braine, dangerous to the Lungs, and in the blacke stinking fume thereof, neerest resembling the horrible Stigian smoke of the pit that is bottomelesse.

King James I was smart enough to know that because of the immense popularity of tobacco among his people, he couldn't ban it outright. Instead, he imposed heavy taxes, amounting to almost 4000 percent, on the importation of tobacco from foreign lands, which included England's own settlements in the New World. And most of that 4000 percent tax on tobacco went directly to his coffers. He went even further to ban the cultivation of tobacco on English soil, and thereby requiring that all tobacco would remain subject to an importation tax. He was so against tobacco and its cultivation on English soil that he reiterated that ban on his deathbed.

His heir, King Charles I, was very similar to his father, and he continued the high taxes and ban on tobacco. His ban on local cultivation read:

The plant or drug called tobacco scarce known to this nation in former times, was in this age first brought into this realm in small quantity, as medicine, and so used...but in the process of time, to satisfy the inordinate appetites of men and women it hath been brought in great quantity, and taken for wantonness and excess, provoking them to drinking and other incontinence, to the great impairing of their healths and depraving them of their manners, so that the care which His Majesty hath of this people hath enforced him to think of some means of preventing of the evil consequences of this immoderate use thereof.

Charles I was more of a believer of a monarch's divine right than his father and went further in his local tobacco bans. He sent his soldiers to hunt out illegal fields (there were many in England at the time because of the high demand) and burn as many as they could. It was not a popular tactic with tobacco users, though, because it increased the price of a much-desired commodity. Charles I also backed expensive wars against Spain, plus two conflicts against Scotland, all of which ended badly for England.

As a way to pay for these wars, and to ensure the kingdom wouldn't go bankrupt, he increased taxes on many things, including tobacco. His popularity plummeted, and—with his armies on the brink of failure—the English Civil War broke out in 1642. It lasted about seven years, ending with King Charles I being beheaded. The Commonwealth of England was formed, and for the next 10 years England was without a king. The Commonwealth wasn't great for tobacco growers. The replacement government continued with the taxes and introduced new laws called the Navigation Acts, which slowed down the shipments of supplies and other goods to the Americas. In addition, the Commonwealth prevented the colonial tobacco growers from selling their wares to any buyers except customers in England.

Despite these obstacles, tobacco grower John Rolfe and many others had huge plantations of tobacco, thousands upon thousands of acres in size. They became extremely wealthy, and throughout a large part of the English colonies in the Americas, especially in Virginia and the Carolinas, tobacco was used as currency.

Even though Rolfe and his later counterparts had learned how to grow and cure tobacco, it was still a serious challenge to meet the demand from England. Tobacco farming and curing is extremely labor intensive, and there weren't enough colonists to work on these ever-expanding farms. The English began to use local labor, abducting and enslaving American Natives to do all the hard work. But the Natives weren't pliable enough slaves. Because of their ability to survive in their natural environment, they escaped easily. Hunting down these escaped slaves was difficult because the Natives knew how to travel quickly through the lands around the plantations. And because these plantations were surrounded by lands occupied by more Natives, it was often impossible for the search party to determine which ones were the escaped slaves and which ones had signed treaties with the English.

When some English plantation bosses began to get too ruthless in their treatment of their Native American slaves, there were two possible outcomes. The first possibility was that the slaves just gave up and died. Many preferred death to enduring overly harsh treatment. The second possibility was attack from other, free Natives who had heard about the brutal treatment. Even though the English were becoming more and more established in the Americas, the local Native population was still much larger and better armed. If a plantation owner angered too many Natives, his plantation could be burned to the ground, and he and his associates could be killed or turned into slaves by the Natives.

A New Source of Labor

Earlier in the century, sometime in 1619, two English pirate ships, the *White Lion* and the *Treasurer*, pulled into Fort Monroe, Virginia. Sailing under Dutch flags to confuse their enemies, they had recently captured a number of African slaves from a Portuguese ship bound for Mexico. The pirates were in need of repair and supplies, and Fort Monroe needed strong workers, so the settlers traded food and services for about 30 African slaves. These slaves were immediately put to work in the tobacco fields.

The Africans were treated in the same way as many of the other colonists and settlers arriving in the British colonies: as indentured servants. They worked as slaves with no pay, but for only a limited period of time, usually about seven years. Then they were set free, given the use of some land and supplies by their previous owners and allowed to prosper as freemen. This was not an unusual arrangement for the time; in fact, most of the people in the English colonies had arrived as indentured servants. The work was difficult, the treatment could be harsh, and death from overwork or mistreatment was common, but for many it was no different than life back in England. The difference in the Americas was that there was the possibility that one day they would be free to work for themselves and given the land and supplies to do so.

More slaves were brought from Africa, and for a period, many of them did work as indentured servants and were set free after their time of service was completed. But many of the wealthier landowners grew tired of this arrangement. They didn't like giving their land away to people who were once their servants, and they didn't like it that once someone was freed, they had to find a replacement worker.

Also, life in England was improving, which meant that fewer and fewer English wanted to go to the colonies. The cost of transportation had also increased, so people had to work longer to gain their freedom.

There had been a rebellion of small farmers, most of whom had been indentured servants, who were against the governor of Virginia and his more friendly policy toward the local Native population. The farmers wanted to expand their farms and wanted the governor to push the Native settlements farther into the wilderness. The rebellion lasted several months, and although it was put down by the English militia, it resulted in the burning of Jamestown and the deaths of many people—English, African and Native.

The Bacon Rebellion, as this event was called, frightened the ruling class of the British colonies. They determined that they had to find a better way to get workers without all the difficulties that indentured servitude provided.

Therefore, when the next shipment of African slaves came over, their slavery was not for a limited period of time, but for the rest of their lives. And if they had families, they would also be slaves. Virginia passed its slave code in 1705, stating that slaves would be people imported from nations that were not Christian, most of them African. And, for many decades, most of these slaves worked on tobacco plantations.

African American workers, mostly women, sort tobacco at the T.B. Williams Tobacco Co., in Richmond, Virginia

Slavery such as this is a key part of United States history. It was so popular among landowners that, by 1790, not long after the United States declared its independence from England, nearly one-fifth of the population of the United States—well over 600,000 people—were slaves.

At the time the American Civil War began in 1860 (slavery being the major reason behind the conflict), nearly four million African slaves lived in the United States.

Slavery is the defining element in relations between African Americans and the population descended from Europeans. That African Americans were slaves for such a long time led to prolonged periods of institutional racism and discrimination against them in the U.S. Even though they had been legally free since the Civil War, it took many decades before they were allowed to vote. For almost a century, African Americans continued to be, at least to some degree, treated as second-class citizens rather than being allowed to participate as equals. They were subject to segregation, reduced opportunities for education and economic prosperity and acts of racial violence, such as rape and lynching.

Despite the 2009 election of Barrack Obama as America's first African American president, significant areas of the United States remain divided along racial lines.

Slavery, which began hundreds of years ago because of tobacco, is a major wound from which the United States has yet to fully heal.

Making Smoking Simpler

The rest of the world quickly took to tobacco, from Russia to Australia, Southeast Asia to South Africa. And although it was very popular, it was only with the invention of the cigarette that tobacco use spread to a large part of the population.

Many Native American peoples had long been smoking tobacco in a manner resembling a cigarette: by rolling up the leaves to form a cylinder and then lighting one end. And many other cultures throughout the world adopted that habit. The French liked the concept and came up with the term *cigarette*, or "little cigar," around 1830. The French tobacco monopoly even began producing cigarettes in 1845. But during the Crimean War of 1853–56, British soldiers adopted and popularized an idea used by their Turkish allies. The Turks, lacking a good leaf in which to roll their tobacco, began using strips of newspaper instead.

The British took the idea home, but no one in England was prepared to manufacture such things. Around the same time in Egypt, however, there were many foreign tobacco merchants and manufacturers. Most were Greeks who had fled their home country because of the Ottoman Empire, which ruled Greece at the time, and they had a monopoly on tobacco production. Some of these merchants started manufacturing cigarettes in Egypt and exporting them to Europe. Egyptian cigarettes became very fashionable and popular in Europe for about 40 years, until the end of World War I, becoming what many people cite as one of the first examples of globally traded manufactured goods.

Even then, cigarettes still weren't as widespread as they are today. They became almost ubiquitous in the West and other parts of the world because of the two world wars. In both these wars, cigarettes were included in the rations of soldiers of many Allied countries. And as soldiers traveled, they traded cigarettes with the locals.

By the end of World War II, a large number of people in Western countries such as Canada, the United States, England and France were smokers. Desire for the habit was fueled even more as almost every form of popular culture—movies, television, literature, comic books, pulp novels—featured smoking as a desirable activity. Smoking one's first cigarette became a right of passage in many cultures.

Health Effects

The World Health Organization (WHO) estimates that 1.3 billion people around the world are regular smokers, making tobacco the most consumed product on the planet. Even though most North Americans and Europeans are now more health conscious and aware of the hazards of smoking tobacco, the U.S. remains one of the largest consumers of cigarettes in the world. Americans smoke a total of 360 billion cigarettes per year.

The Chinese, however, smoke over 1.6 trillion cigarettes per year (slightly more per capita than the Americans), and the WHO estimates that 1.3 million Chinese die annually from tobacco-related diseases. That's equivalent to the entire population of the city of San Diego. Japan leads the world in per-capita smoking, with each Japanese person smoking an equivalent of 2600 cigarettes every year. Not surprisingly, smoking is the leading cause of death in Japan today and is responsible for 20 percent of its cancers.

The health impact of tobacco through cigarette smoking is indeed incredible. The WHO estimates that smoking can reduce a person's life expectancy by 25 years and that a person dies of a tobacco-related illness every 6.3 seconds. By the end of this century, the WHO estimates one billion people will have died prematurely because of smoking.

But even with these statistics, there are still many advocates for the powers of tobacco.

"For over five centuries, tobacco has been integrated into cultures as diverse as mankind itself, each of which has evolved justifications for using the weed, some ancient, others original," writes Iain Gately.

> *Although tobacco has lost most of its religious associations, many of the oldest reasons for smoking are still in use, and still valid. Tobacco has recently been discovered to protect against some of the most*

devastating ailments of old age, including Alzheimer's disease and Parkinson's disease. It has also been shown to guard against cancer of the womb. As to tobacco's association with contemplation and thought, there are centuries of precedents of eminent smokers, who cannot be dismissed as simply victims of their ages or habits. Many great men and women have left elegant testimonies to their tobacco habits, which will be joined, I believe, with others made in centuries to come.

Gately's comments are European in their nature in that they argue in favor of tobacco because of some possible practical uses and its use and support by great personalities from the past. To many Aboriginal communities, tobacco doesn't need such support, it is just, with some minor differences, the same sacred weed it has been for millennia. Many aboriginal societies did—and continue to—use tobacco recreationally and suffered the same health effects as the rest of the users throughout the world. But they also lament the corruption of their sacred weed and the damage it has caused. The commercial uses of tobacco are not the preferred use of tobacco. Tobacco is considered a gift from the Creator, and, in return, man must treat it as such.

In many aboriginal communities throughout North America, tobacco remains a sacred weed, integral to many ceremonies and rituals, such as sweats, smudges and many others. It is also a gift given to the Creator and Mother Earth in these ceremonies or to people involved in these ceremonies or as a gift to newcomers. But tobacco as a gift is not just something to be smoked; it's a sign of respect for the person and for their shared knowledge.

According to Cree Elder Vern Harper, as quoted in a paper written by University of Toronto PhD student Lynn Lavallee, "We are spirits living in the human experience. Tobacco helps us communicate with the spirit world and the Great Spirit. Tobacco helps us communicate with others, particularly when meeting for the purposes of sharing and healing."

But tobacco wasn't the only crop from the Americas that has had a significant social and political impact on the world.

Chapter Thirteen

Maize

In the 1954 movie *Apache*, a young warrior named Massai refuses to accept Geronimo's surrender to the United States Army. So while en route to a reservation in Florida, he escapes, hoping to return to his homeland in New Mexico. In the movie, Massai makes his way back across the country chased by an evil white bounty hunter but finally arrives home. He falls in love with the daughter of the new chief and hopes to settle down. The people talk about becoming farmers and planting this new crop that the Cherokee are now growing. They learned about this crop from the white man, and the Apache are told that if they learn how to grow this crop and settle down, they will no longer have to fear the white man.

After some adventures, falling in love and fighting a guerilla war against the white man, Massai finally realizes that the only way he can save his family is to become a farmer and grow this new white-man crop: corn, also known as maize.

Given that this is a 1950s Hollywood production, it no doubt contains many inaccuracies and blunders. The least of these flaws were the casting of an Irish Protestant, Burt Lancaster, as the Apache warrior Massai, former beauty pageant queen Jean Peters as Massai's love interest, Nalini, and Lithuanian American actor Charles Bronson as Hondo, an Apache warrior out to get Massai. In fact, out of all the actors in this movie, none of the Native American characters are actually played by Native Americans.

But that wasn't the worst of it.

Probably the most egregious error or flagrant disregard for actual history (no doubt another piece of American historical propaganda) in this movie is the claim that the white man taught the Natives about corn and how to grow it.

It is this kind of myth that perpetuates the notion that the Native people of the Americas were primitive hunters and gatherers who needed the assistance of the "intellectually superior" white man to help them become civilized and thus better citizens.

All of these notions are false. Corn did not come from Europe. The white Europeans did not bring it to the "savage" Native American tribes to help them become more civilized.

The Apache did not need to learn how to grow corn from the Europeans because, centuries before Columbus set off from Europe, they had already been cultivating it. It was one of their staple foods. Indeed, corn is a crop native to the Americas that was cultivated by most North American, Mesoamerican, South American and Caribbean cultures.

When the Europeans arrived in the "New World," they had never heard of corn. To them it was a foreign plant, and they had no idea how to grow, harvest or even eat it.

But the Natives of the Americas taught the Europeans all they knew about corn, and in no time it became one of the most widely used plants in the entire world. Now, based on harvest weight, corn is the number one crop in the world.

The Earliest Maize

No one really knows for sure who was the first group to start cultivating maize. The oldest cobs of maize found in the Americas were a group of over 23,000 primitive cobs found in a series of five caves in the Tehuacán region in the southwestern corner of what is now Mexico. These cobs were estimated to be between 6000 and 8000 years old. But some surmised that maize cultivation goes as far back in the Americas as 10,000 years ago.

The most popular theory is that maize was first cultivated in Central America and then spread to South America, initially into Peru some 6000 years ago. And then it quickly reached Ecuador, Chile and Argentina. Over two millennia before the birth of Christ, possibly earlier, maize had spread through most of Central and South America.

Maize also began to make its way north, beginning along the Rio Grande. The Rio Grande is the fourth-largest river system in the United States, stretching over 1800 miles from its source in southwestern Colorado through New Mexico and Texas, and then becoming the border between the U.S. and Mexico before emptying out into the Gulf of Mexico.

For thousands of years, the land along the Rio Grande and its many tributaries was a vibrant area, home to a wide variety of peoples that included the San Dieguito-Pinto, who lived from 6500 BC until 200 AD; the Oshara, who lived from 5500 BC until 600 AD; the Cochise, from before 5000 BC until 200 BC; the Chihuahua, from 6000 BC until 250 AD; plus what many call the Oasisamerica cultures, who existed from 3500 BC until 1300 AD. These Oasisamerica cultures include the Hohokam, the Mogollon, the Fremont, the Patayan and the fabled Anasazi.

Living in the region of the Four Corners, the area where the states of Colorado, Utah, New Mexico and Arizona meet, the Anasazi is one of the most studied of all North American cultures. During the earlier years of their development, the Anasazi took to living in caves and rocky shelters. A hundred or so years later, they started building their first subterranean cities, with up to four adobe houses arranged in a circle.

Later on, the Anasazi developed ceramics and wide-ranging irrigation systems. They also started using masonry, which resulted in great works of architecture and multi-story dwellings with the development of ceramics.

But by the 13th century, the Anasazi had abandoned their great cities and faded away, mostly migrating to other areas of the southwest, becoming the ancestors of the modern Pueblo people. No one really knows why the Anasazi left their homes, but many believe a major drought brought this civilization to its knees. During their time, however, the Anasazi were great cultivators of maize, and it was thanks to them that corn spread northward up the Rio Grande.

From the Rio Grande, maize then made its way farther north, east and west, so that within a few centuries, it became the most cultivated crop for the Native peoples of the Americas. It was grown along the eastern coast of the United States, as far north as the St. Lawrence River. Tribes in the Dakotas grew it, and so did those living along the Mississippi, west to Kansas and Nebraska, and, as started earlier, in the southwestern United States and south all the through Central and South America.

Planting Systems and Empires

Most nations didn't grow maize by itself. It was part of a trio of crops—maize, beans and squash—that many Native groups called the "Three Sisters." The concept, called companion farming, or *milpa* (to use a Maya term), was simple yet ingenious.

The maize was planted first and left to grow until the stalks were about six inches tall. Then the beans and the squash were planted intermittently around the maize. As the maize grew taller and taller, it provided something for the beans to climb. And the leaves of the squash spread low along the ground, creating a blanket to block sunlight from reaching the ground, thus preventing weeds from growing or spreading. The beans and the squash also provided nutrients that fertilized the maize and helped it to grow even higher and to produce a better harvest.

The milpa techniques ensured that the soil would remain more fertile than with any mono-cultivation. If used properly, a single milpa field could sustain crops for over 20 years. And then, when the crops were rotated, the recovery time for a field was much faster.

Hopi Indian girls grinding corn at Shonghopavi, Arizona. Corn, normally grown with beans and squash, was the staple food for Natives throughout North and South America.

These agriculture techniques were so successful that milpa became the most widely used agriculture practice throughout the Americas. Many cultures didn't limit themselves to just three crops, sometimes planting dozens, including various types of peppers, avocados, tomatoes, sweet potatoes, melons and other grains.

Although many of these other crops were grown, maize became the predominant crop of most Native American peoples. Some groups were so successful in its cultivation that their societies grew in size and became empires that could match any other empire in the history of humankind.

Empires fueled by maize included the Maya and Aztecs of Mexico and parts of Central America, the Incas of Peru and the Andean plateau, and the Hopewell tradition on the lands along the Mississippi River.

Sometime between 3500 BC and 1800 BC, the Maya rose from a series of settlements to become one of the most enduring Mesoamerican civilizations. Maize was their predominant crop. During their pre-Classic period, the Maya were mostly a group of small, hierarchical states, though a few larger states demanded fealty over a much greater area. But, over time, the Maya became one of the predominant cultures in the Americas, their influence still seen today in the cultures of Mexico (even the north), Guatemala, Honduras and El Salvador.

During its Classic period, the Maya civilization rivaled any other in the world with its art and culture, science, architecture, agricultural techniques, administration, food supply chains and trade. Many times, they surpassed it. Although the cities of the Maya never reached the size and scope of the Aztec capitals of Tenochtitlan, Texcoco and Tlacopan (cities with great pyramids and urban areas larger than London, Paris and many other world cities of the period), the Maya were a highly sophisticated culture.

As mentioned earlier (in the chapter about the Great Law of Peace), the Maya developed the concept of zero centuries before the Europeans adopted the concept from the Hindus. And their calendars, which followed solar years, were much more accurate than the calendar used by Europeans at the time.

The Dresden Codex, a complete 11th- or 12th-century copy of an earlier Maya codex, has astronomical tables that many experts consider to be the most accurate for the time. The codex contains almanacs, astronomical and astrological tables, and religious comments, and among its uses were predicting the weather, floods and favorable growing times, especially for maize, There are also many medical references on how to prevent and treat illness and injury.

Modern Europeans started developing and using this kind of almanac around the 12th century AD. Its origins may be similar to the ones used by the Ancient Greeks a few centuries before Christ, but their focus was mostly astronomical with a bit of astrology added. The Babylonians, around the 8th century BC, also had astronomical tables and statistics, and many Arab countries had something like an almanac around the turn of the first millennium AD.

Roger Bacon was one of the first to use the word "almanac," in 1287 AD. And because the word doesn't seem to have any roots in Arabic, Latin or other older languages, some historians suggest that the almanac—as an annual publication that includes weather forecasts, planting dates, astronomical information, tide tables, as well as other information—is entirely a Western European invention.

But the Maya and their ancestors, the Olmecs, were using detailed almanacs around 2500 years before Christ, which shows that just because one society determines a name for something and that name manages to become the primary descriptive word for it, it doesn't automatically mean that society invented it.

To grow their maize, the Maya (along with the Aztecs, the Incas of South America and the Hopewells of North America) used milpa fields, raised fields, terraces and forest gardens. They also developed one of the most unusual maize cultivation techniques, the *chinampa*.

A chinampa was an artificial island—or floating garden, as it has been called—that was created by staking out a section of a lake, a swamp or an estuary and then fencing it off using wattle (a mesh of woven sticks). Once the water was drained from the area, each planting bed thus created was raised using mud, sediment from the lake and decaying vegetation, which eventually made the beds higher than the level of the lake. Trees planted at the corners of these islands secured the land, and small canals of water flowed between each pair of islands. Once the land was ready, the Maya cultivated it like any milpa field, planting a collection of crops, the most popular being maize.

The advantage of a chinampa was that it could grow more maize and other crops in a smaller space than the average milpa field. Many of them yielded three crops per year, which was very significant as the population of the Maya Empire increased over the centuries.

Each chinampa field was about 100 feet long by eight feet wide, and the Maya had massive areas of land with 50, 100 or even more chinampas in one area. Chinampas were so successful that the Aztecs, close neighbors and trading partners with the Maya, had a series of chinampa farms encircling their great capital city of Tenochtitlan. These fields allowed Tenochtitlan to become the largest city in ancient Mexico.

During its peak, Tenochtitlan had an area of more than eight square miles and a population of 200,000. When compared to many other cities of the same time, Tenochtitlan was one of the greatest. The average population of a large city in Europe at the same time was 50,000 to 100,000. London was the largest city in medieval Europe, reaching 100,000. But the Black Plague cut most of the population throughout Europe by a third. So, by the time Columbus had reached America, London's population was only one-quarter that of Tenochtitlan, and most European cities, even the great ones, were smaller in size. In fact, out of all the cities of the world at the time, only a few in China matched the size and scope of Tenochtitlan.

But by the time the Aztec Empire had reached its height of power, around the 12th and 13th centuries AD, the Maya civilization had declined. They didn't die off (Maya still exist in Central America), but they abandoned their city states and faded into the background.

Maize was extremely important and powerful to the Maya, and it was the key component in their creation myth. According to the *Popul Vuh*, the "book of the community" from one of the Maya kingdoms in Guatemala, after "the Maker" and the Hero Twins of Tepeu and Gucumatz made the world, they made animals and also tried to make human creatures, first out of mud. These first humans soaked up water and dissolved. So then they tried wood. But wood had no power; these men had no souls and lacked speech and intelligence.

As the book relates:

After that they began to talk about the creation and the making of our first mother and father; of yellow corn and of white corn they made their flesh; of corn meal dough they made the arms and the legs of man. Only dough of corn meal went into the flesh of our first fathers, the four men, who were created.... And as they had the appearance of men, they were men; they talked, conversed, saw and heard, walked, grasped things; they were good and handsome men, and their figure was the figure of a man.

So the Maya made regular offerings to the other world and various gods. Many of these offerings included maize, as a special bread, a drink made of 415 grains of parched maize for a New Year blessing, or a burning of exactly 49 grains for another ceremony.

The Aztecs also included maize in their creation myth, with human beings formed out of maize dough, and it was because of the life-giving power of maize that they were able to live. They even had two gods of maize. The first was Cinteotl, the god of maize, and the second was Xilonen (also known as Chicomecoatl)—the goddess of tender maize.

Maize was key to many important rituals of the Aztecs. At the beginning of the harvest, they had a group of older women each pick five newly ripened maize cobs. These cobs were then wrapped up and carried on the backs of these women, the same way a newborn child was wrapped and carried. The women carried these cobs to a destination, usually their home or the home of a family member or friend, and placed the cobs into a special basket. The cobs remained in the basket until the following year, to represent the resting of the maize spirits until the next harvest.

Maize Changes Parts of Europe, China and Africa

Obviously, when the Europeans arrived in the Americas, they had no choice but to notice all the maize. It was everywhere. Conquistadors spoke of fields filled with crops as "tall as soldier's spikes." And they marveled at the elaborate systems used to grow the corn and were thunderstruck by the concept that this maize was also used as currency, much in the manner of gold. In fact, the first Europeans to land in the Americas, the Spaniards, were stunned to realize that these Native Americans paid more reverence to maize than they did to gold.

And although gold from the Americas helped fuel and expand the Spanish Empire, such success was only short-lived. The gold of the Spanish Empire faded with time, but the introduction of maize changed Europe and other parts of the world in even deeper ways.

At first, many Europeans believed that maize was an inferior and less nutritional crop than traditional grains, such as wheat and barley. For some reason, maize was called "Turkish wheat," "Turkish grain," even "Spanish wheat." But it spread quickly, mostly because it grew in areas that didn't compete with traditional crops. It was also much hardier than the wheat and barley of Europe, could be harvested sooner and consistently produced higher yields. Yet, despite all these positive aspects of maize, most Europeans, at least in the first few centuries of corn's introduction, believed it was suitable only for animal feed or for people of the lowest economic standing.

One of the most popular ways these poor folks could eat maize was developed in northern Italy. The Italians mixed maize with water to create a sort of porridge, *polenta*, as they called it.

Nowadays, polenta is a classic Italian food dish that is served in many ways.

Over time, maize became the key ingredient in the daily bread of Serbia, Romania and Moldavia. It became a major force for political and social change in these countries as well. For centuries, Serbian and Greek peasants, especially those who lived in the mountains, suffered from the effects of little food. Because of this, their population remained static, and they were susceptible to many diseases. As a result, they did not have the numbers or the strength to effect any major social or political change on the totalitarian monarchies that then existed. According to Maslow's hierarchy of needs, physiological needs (involved with survival) always come first. A human must breathe, have enough water and food for oneself and one's family, find adequate shelter for the same and ensure the propagation of the species. And when those physiological needs are unmet or constantly at risk, then humans have no time nor desire to seek to satisfy their other needs, such as for safety from unilateral control or belonging to a broader social group than one's family or village.

For these reasons, when maize was introduced to the region around 1830, most peasants in Greece and Serbia were still focusing on their survival needs rather than their need to effect change.

Many of these people lived in the mountain regions for the warmest parts of the year, but in winter, the weather forced them to make their way to the lowlands and more urban areas, which were under the control of the Ottoman Empire. And the empire considered the mountain people to be a drain on their resources. So these people had to constantly pay fealty to the governing leaders to ensure their basic survival. The lowland areas were also filled with mosquitoes, and those mosquitoes carried malaria, a disease that took a major toll on the people.

With the arrival of maize, things changed. Because maize was an adaptive crop and could be successfully grown at higher altitudes, the people living in these areas did not have to move in winter. They now had a stable food source they could control, which meant their population increased. Their children grew stronger as a result of the regular access to maize and the other foods grown with it, so they were less susceptible to disease and lived longer. And the stable food source allowed these people to move up the ladder in the hierarchy of needs. So over time, they had the desire and the need to feel part of a larger group and to effect change in their lives outside their basic survival needs.

In the words of noted world historian William McNeill in 1991:

> *When Greeks, Serbs and Vlasch found that the new maize crop allowed them to live all year round in the high mountain valleys, where they were safe from the twin scourges of the plains—malaria and Turkish oppression—the political and economic balance of the Balkans began to shift.... Thus one may say that what potatoes did for Germany and Russia between 1700 and 1914, maize did for the mountain Greeks and Serbs in the same period of time. In each case, a new and far more productive food resource allowed population to surpass older limits, and larger populations in turn provided the basis for the enhanced political and military power attained by the four peoples involved.*

Despite the change it brought to the Balkans, in other parts of Europe, maize was initially seen as an interesting crop but not a major food source for average folks. Today, Europe grows almost 84 million tons of maize every year.

Maize was introduced in China, perhaps by the Portuguese, between 1520 and 1560 but, if not, then by the Dutch, who controlled much of the trade between Europe and Asia after that time.

The new food revolutionized agriculture in that Oriental empire. As in Europe, at first maize was seen by the Chinese as a food suitable only for peasants. But maize allowed the growing of crops in many areas that were unsuitable for other Chinese staples, such as rice and wheat. Such areas included the inlands hills of the Yangtze Delta, where overpopulation and famine were serious problems. In the more mountainous regions of Yunan and Szechuan, most peasants had to work in low-paying and dangerous jobs. Many had neither the time nor the money to even consider starting a family. And if they did, they had no real control over their sources of food, so the mortality rate among children was high.

But corn allowed these laborers to cultivate land in areas that were previously seen as worthless, where traditional crops could not be grown. So instead of being laborers all their lives, generation after generation, millions of people became farmers. Their populations also increased, in many case doubling and tripling in a short period of time. And with an increased population and a stable source of food, many Chinese peasants became dissatisfied with what they saw as a corrupt government.

At the time of maize's introduction to China, the Ming Dynasty was at the height of its reign. A few generations later, the Ming Dynasty's 300-year rule over China was overthrown by the Manchus, who, over a period of over 20 years, started and expanded a rebellion against the Ming emperor. Many of the increased population of dissatisfied peasants joined the Manchu rebellion. On May 26, 1644, the Manchu army entered the capital of Beijing and took over the city and a large part of the country. Zhu Youjian, the last true emperor of the Ming Dynasty, hanged himself from a tree in a courtyard of the Forbidden Palace.

Maize is still the number one crop grown in China today, and that country is the world's second largest producer of maize, with over 230 million tons produced every year.

According to Betty Fussell in her book *The Story of Corn*, maize "helped to extend and sustain the power of the Manchu invaders who overthrew the last of the Ming emperors in the mid-seventeenth century." The Manchus went on to rule China from 1644 to 1912.

No one really knows who first imported maize into Africa, possibly the Portuguese, but it could have been various representatives of the Ottoman Empire, who also got maize from the Portuguese. But the impact of maize on that continent was even more astonishing. And not all the developments were positive.

Unlike traditional Africa crops of the time, maize could be grown in a wide range of places: in coastal areas, on the savannahs and plains, in the mountains, in forests and in the transition areas between these regions

Maize was also an ideal first crop, a crop that was grown on an area recently cleared of trees. Also, according to James C. McCann is his book *Maize and Grace: Africa's Encounter with a New World Crop*:

> Maize's capacity to provide a second harvest in a single season was a strategic boost to local food supply. This food supply, in turn, released labor to push the frontiers of forest settlement forward and support development of the art of politics and statecraft. The forest fallow crop repertoire as a whole was thus part of an agricultural transformation that drew new labor into the forest and broke the logjam of primary clearance. One of the engines that pushed the Upper Guinea "forest fallow" revolution was the arrival of three New World domestic plants that occupied strategic niches in forest cultivation. As a new cultigen, maize offered an advantage—it was an early-maturing food source that provided carbohydrates by the end of the rains, with less work than yams.
>
> Maize also gave a second harvest, while cassava—another low-labor (but long maturing) crop, which was able to remain stored in the ground for extended periods—complemented maize's early yield and double crops. It is therefore not surprising that historical sources report the increasing dominance of maize in forest and coastal cultivation during the era of the slave trade.

Support for the slave trade was an unfortunate consequence of maize's increased usage in Africa and the resulting increased population, especially in West Africa, where maize was initially produced. More people in Africa meant more slaves from

Africa. And maize was a quick and easy way to feed the slaves while they were being held in Africa and on the arduous trip across the Atlantic.

But the introduction of maize had additional positive effects. The online Encyclopedia of Food and Culture notes that in *Africa's Emerging Maize Revolution*, by Derek Byerlee and Carl Eicher, the authors agree that:

> [T]*he adoption of maize has been the primary engine driving the transformation of the African social, political, and economic landscape for the many societies that have been swept up in this new agricultural revolution.*
>
> *More specifically, it is becoming increasingly evident that those agricultural practices identified with maize, such as swidden cultivation, extensive or shifting settlement patterns that are, in turn, identified with swidden systems, the processing of maize with basalt grinding slabs, the female domination of these labor-intensive food processing and storage traditions, and the emerging role of women in the maize-dominated marketplace have all played significant roles in the transformation of the African political economy. Moreover, given the fact that in many areas of Africa, much of the traditional African agricultural complex—centered on such crops as millet—has been displaced by maize has much to do with the changing face of African cuisine at the most fundamental level of analysis, and more*

generally, at the interface of cultural change and transformation…

[N]o African country has remained untouched by the diffusion and exchange of maize, and the agricultural practices on the African continent range from the simple sowing of maize kernels along rivers and streams to the cultivation of maize in household gardens. While widespread, these traditional practices are primitive compared to the magnitude and intensity of agribusiness development and investment in commercially viable maize agricultural field systems.

Today, the continent of Africa grows over 56 million tons of maize per year.

Learning to Grow Maize in the Colonies

Back in North America, maize played a key role in the European settlement of that continent. Native tribes offered maize to settlers in Jamestown and to the pilgrims who mythically landed on Plymouth Rock. They also taught them how to grow it themselves, and many historians say that, without this help, these settlers would have starved and the political and social landscape of North America today might be completely different.

The first governor of the Plymouth Colony, William Bradford, said once, "And sure it was God's good providence that we found this corne [sic], for we know not how else we should have done." Although he mentioned the importance of corn for saving his settlement, he (or history) seemed to have forgotten the people who gave it to them.

As the 13 British colonies became the United States and more Europeans came across the Atlantic to settle in the "New World," maize became even more important. Because the eastern parts of the country were already well populated with immigrants and their offspring, more and more people headed west, into the wilds of Ohio, Kansas, Iowa, Illinois and other states that are now part of the Midwestern United States. Maize was the principal crop of these areas, the initial crop that these new settlers planted and the one that sustained them. Unfortunately for the original inhabitants, the success of these settlers sparked even more European settlement, and over time, the people who had initially lived on this land and who had also grown maize on this land, the Native Americans, were slowly pushed out.

Maize Today

Maize, or corn as most Americans call it, is now the number one crop grown in America, with over 333 million tons produced every year. In some states, such as Iowa, corn is almost the only crop grown.

Throughout the world, over 393 million acres of maize are grown annually, with a yield of 817 million tons. Maize is the most widely used crop; it is not only eaten on the cob, from a can or bag of kernels or in a porridge similar to polenta, but it is also processed in countless ways. It is distributed to livestock as feed, it is processed into drinks, and it is pounded into tortillas with techniques very similar to those used by early Mesoamericans.

Corn starch or corn flour is an important ingredient in home cooking and in a variety of industrialized food products. Maize can be processed to yield corn oil, which has a multitude of uses. The starch of maize can be used to make syrups, particularly high-fructose corn syrup, which is a ubiquitous sweetener used not only in candy products and soda drinks but also in a wide range of other processed foods. Grain alcohol made from maize is traditionally the source of bourbon whiskey, and maize is sometimes used to make beer.

Corn starch is used to make fabrics, plastics, glues and other chemical products. Maize and its derivatives are now found in over 1000 products in the average supermarket. Corn has also recently been touted as a possible source of renewable fuel to replace nonrenewable fossil fuels for cars, buses and other forms of modern transportation.

Finally, some species of maize are used as popcorn (see Appendix), which is still one of the most popular snacks in North America. Almost every single Native American nation that grew maize also had popcorn. The Natives taught the Europeans how to make it. For many years, popcorn wasn't overly popular in North America. Then came the Great Depression of the 1930s and World War II. Because popcorn was much cheaper than other snacks and, during the war, sugar rationing lowered candy production, Americans started eating more and more popcorn. Today, popcorn is a major part of modern culture, eaten primarily while watching movies or at sporting events.

But Wait, There's More

Maize is now widely grown, under a wide range of conditions in many places between 58 degrees north latitude in Canada and Russia and 40 degrees south latitude in South America.

It is the most studied plant species on the planet.

A poster promoting the importance of corn, although it fails to mention that corn came from Native Americans.

But the story of maize and how the Native Americans grew it and then passed it on to the Europeans so it could change many parts of the world is not the entire story. The history of maize and Native Americans has a much more significant and fascinating aspect to it.

Maize is an important cereal, like rice, wheat, millet, barley and other similar crops. Many early tribes of hunting and gathering humans collected these grains for food. But one of the key differences between maize and most other cereal crops is that with the other crops (such as wild wheat and barley), the grain is at the top of the stem, where it is readily available to be collected.

Unlike many major cereal crops, the seeds of maize do not grow on the top of the plant and are not easily distributed by the death of the plant or by wind or other weather elements. The kernels of maize are wrapped in thick husks. Unless humans harvest these husks and tear them open to get to the kernels inside and then plant them, they won't have much of a chance to reproduce.

When most grain plants start to die at the end of the season, the seeds fall to the ground and may be spread by wind and rain. In this way, these plants can self-propagate to expand their range. People learned to harvest these seeds for food, and when they began to realize that new plants could grow from them, they decided to plant some for themselves.

It is strongly believed that this discovery prompted what is called the Neolithic Revolution, the point in humanity's history at which our ancestors transformed from a mostly hunting and gathering society to one that used agriculture. Over time, these agricultural societies became more settled and gave rise to villages and larger towns. They developed separation of labor, modified the natural environment through irrigation and invented food storage techniques. They developed trade between groups and created more advanced notions of art, architecture, culture, writing, numbering systems and political structures. The Neolithic Revolution set the stage for the development of civilizations in key areas, for example, the first Sumerian cities of the Middle East (around 3500 BC), which are said to be the origins of Western civilization.

The Neolithic Revolution occurred independently in six areas throughout the world over a period extending from about 10,000 to 7000 years ago. The earliest ones are said to have occurred in southwestern and southern Asia, northern and central Africa and in Central America.

In many areas of the world known for the first civilizations, the original crops cultivated were species such as millet, rice and wheat. In Central America, the key crop was maize. The other cereals have wild ancestors that many human groups were already harvesting and eating as hunter-gatherers. But no definitive wild ancestor plant to maize has yet been found. Many people believe, though, that maize is a descendant of a wild Central American grass called teosinte.

Teosinte does not look much like maize and, unlike the wild ancestors to rice and wheat, has little nutritional value. Grown wild, teosinte produces a head containing only 7–12 hard seeds that together have less nutrition than a single kernel of maize.

But the theory that teosinte is a direct ancestor to modern maize, or even to the primitive strains of maize that have been found at archeological sites, is still strongly debated today.

In the 1930s, a Harvard botanist named Paul C. Mangelsdorf postulated that maize was the natural hybrid of two plants, a wild grass of the genus *Tripsacum* and a now-extinct version of wild maize. Several decades later, an archeological team found a series of five caves in the Tehuacán Valley, in the southwestern corner of what is now Mexico. In these caves, they found over 23,000 primitive maize cobs, as mentioned earlier in this chapter. The cobs and other artifacts nearby were estimated to be around 6000 to 8000 years old. Mangelsdorf worked with the archeological team and declared that these cobs, especially the oldest and the smallest cobs, were the reputed extinct maize cobs he had been talking about and they were the true wild ancestors to corn.

But Mangelsdorf's theory was shot down when later genetic experiments found that these maize cobs and *Tripsacum* had no genetic connection. One scientist, University of Wisconsin botanist Hugh Iltis, noted that the "wild maize" found in the Tehuacán caves was genetically identical to a variety of domestic popcorn from Argentina. So there was no way that these cobs of maize, still cited as the oldest actual cobs of maize found in the world, could be considered wild.

Iltis took his study even further by proposing that because maize is so far removed from teosinte, and because it's impossible that even ancient forms of maize could have propagated themselves, there was only one conclusion to be made: maize was human-made. Subsequently, several other researchers have agreed that maize was created when Native Americans took a mutated version of teosinte (or something similar) and, over several generations of the plant, used relatively sophisticated hybridization techniques to intensively breed out the unfavorable traits of the plant and to breed in the more favorable ones.

The implication is that when other cultures were just learning how to plant and harvest crops sometime between 6000 and 8000 years ago, maybe even earlier, Native Americans in north Central America were already crossbreeding different varieties of similar plants in order to perfect their crop and to better suit their needs. It appears that they not only understood the basics of simple hereditary genetics—that plants and animals pass on their traits to their descendants—but they were also experimenting with it.

"To get corn out of teosinte is so—you couldn't get a grant to do that now, because it would sound so crazy," said Nina V. Federoff, a geneticist at Pennsylvania State University, as quoted in Charles C. Mann's book *1491: New Revelations of the Americas Before Columbus*. "Somebody who did that today would get a Nobel Prize!"

And it didn't take them that long either. In 1998, geneticists from Rutgers University in New Jersey determined that it would have taken a group of determined and highly knowledgeable group of Native Americans about a decade to create maize from a series of crossbreeding trials with various strains of teosinte and possibly other plants.

Thus, it appears that Native Americans are responsible not only for introducing maize to Europeans and then it becoming one of the most significant agricultural crops in the history of the world, they are also the ones who created it.

It was, as geneticist Federoff wrote in a 2003 issue of the journal *Science*, "arguably man's first and perhaps his greatest, feat of genetic engineering."

We now know that, with the help of maize and tobacco—two crops that changed the world—Native Americans helped rescue English settlers in the Americas and allowed them to thrive. As a result, they were able to create successful colonies and, later on, revolt against their king and create their own new country.

But that was not the only influence Native Americans had on the development of Western civilization in the Americas. Indeed, many scholars believe that ideas for how to set up a new democratic republic in the Americas came from the Natives themselves, via the Iroquois and their Great Law of Peace.

Chapter Fourteen

Government Influences

The Hopewell Tradition

Of course, the Iroquois Confederacy, with their Great Law of Peace, was not the first form of government organization in the Americas.

In North America, nearly 1000 years before the confederacy, there existed the Hopewell tradition, a band of connected societies that ranged from the Atlantic coast of Florida and the Mississippi Delta to north of Lake Superior and the St. Lawrence River.

The Hopewell tradition wasn't a single society ruled by a single government, leader or alliance; instead, it consisted only of an overarching group of similar groups that participated in a massive trade and exchange system that saw goods being traded throughout the Midwest and much of the northern and southern parts of the eastern United States and parts of Canada. Some of these goods came into the system as raw materials from one group that, after they were traded, were transformed by another group into some type of product that, in turn, was put back into the system again.

The Hopewell tradition, which existed from 200 BC to 500 AD, is believed to have developed from the Adena culture, a society of about 300 settlements around what is now part of the U.S. state of Ohio, and then spread through contact and trade with other Native cultures throughout the land.

Although the individual societies in the Hopewell tradition were different from one another, they all had similar systems of government. They had fairly firm hierarchal structures in which specific families, for whatever reason, had higher standing and control in the culture. There were also strong leaders, known as "Big Men," who did not lead as kings or priests but who were men of influence and persuasion able to garner consensus for their viewpoints on a variety of matters.

Many of the societies associated with the Hopewell tradition also developed the practice of mound building, which resulted in large geometric earthworks that are deemed some of the most impressive Native monuments in North America. Some of the mounds are 70 feet high or higher and were built in a pattern about a mile or more long.

No one has really determined why the mounds were built, but some scholars have surmised that they served some ceremonial purpose. Others have noted that the geometric shapes and layout of the mounds point to them being astronomical observatory sites and that their placement reflected the position of the moon, the sun and constellations at various times of the year.

The groups of the Hopewell tradition also gave rise to highly skilled artisans who turned bone, silver, shark teeth, pearls, copper and many other materials into great pieces of art. These pieces they either traded with other groups or used themselves in ceremonial events.

Government Among the Maya, Aztecs and Incas

Around the same the Hopewell tradition was flourishing in North America, Central and South America had their own great civilizations.

The Maya enjoyed their Classic period from 250 AD to 900 AD. Their empire stretched through much of Mexico and Central America. Unlike the Hopewell tradition to the north, the Maya were a rigid hierarchal society, but it was separated into connected city states. Each city or area state was led by a family dynasty that was headed by hereditary leader known as an *ajaw*. Always a male, the ajaw was pretty much the king of a city state; he ruled over all and could command armies, dispense justice and tax the people in any way he saw fit. The ajaw and his family always lived in the center of the city, in plush surroundings near the major temples and pyramids.

Priests were also important power holders in Maya society. And although it is understood that the Maya did practice human sacrifice to their numerous gods, much regarding their religious traditions is still not fully understood by today's scholars.

Even with very strong rulers who had the power of life and death over almost every single citizen, the Maya culture flourished, becoming one of the most important and sophisticated cultures, not just in the Americas but in the entire world. All expressions of Maya culture and science—its art, literature, architecture, science, astronomy, mathematics, medicine, and so on—were among the most advanced of the time.

The Aztecs, whose civilization reigned from the 12th century AD to the 15th century, followed the Maya, and they, too, built a strong, advanced civilization based on powerful, dynastic leadership connected to religious powers. In many ways, the Aztec leadership structures were similar to European monarchies. For example, the strong family in the major capital city of Tenochtitlan kept control and dominated other lesser city states by some use of the military but mostly by installing puppet leaders or creating alliances through marriage. However, the Aztecs were not always interested in exerting supreme power over everyone. When they conquered another city state and assumed power, they pretty much left the system and many of the administrative officials in place, allowing the government to function as it had before. All they asked was that a substantial tribute be paid on a regular basis, and then local affairs were allowed to run without their influence.

Like the Maya, the Aztecs had a social and economic class system, but it was a bit more flexible than European systems. Peasants, a category that included artists and warriors as well as typical laborers and agriculture workers, could rise higher in social class through education and hard work. Slaves could buy their freedom through their savings or by marrying their masters or bearing their children. Slaves could also be set free when their masters died or for performing outstanding deeds.

The Aztec religious system was very powerful, and it, too, involved human sacrifice, even more so than that of the Maya. But this practice was not as frequent and as intense in numbers as many people believe. Aztecs priests were known to inflate their numbers to seem more godlike to the people and their descendants. For example, one priest claimed to have sacrificed more than 84,000 people in less than four days. But many historians believe that just handling the logistics and the physical toll would have made such a feat impossible.

The Inca Empire, which began around the 12th century AD and lasted well into the 16th, also had a sophisticated system of government to help it rule over the largest empire in pre-Columbian history. A truly massive empire, it stretched thousands of miles down the spine of the Andes Mountains, from present-day southern Colombia to southern Chile and into Argentina.

Unlike the Aztecs and the Maya, the Incas had a supreme leader, the Sapa Inca, who lived in the capital city of Cuzco, which is located in today's southeastern Peru, in the Urubamba Valley of the Andes Mountains. The Inca Empire was divided into four regions, which were ruled by governors who answered to the Sapa Inca and also sent tributes to the capital on an annual basis.

The Inca civilization was also a theocracy in which the Sapa Inca was considered to be a direct descendant of Inti, the sun god. All the Sapa Incas in the history of the Inca Empire were members of the same dynasty, descendants of the original Sapa Inca, Manco Cápac. It's no wonder that the Spanish were impressed with the Incas, because their societies were in some ways similar.

Although the Incas, Maya, Aztecs, Hopewell peoples and others created great empires and examples of government-based societies in the Americas, there was another society, much older and much smaller, that has a special place in the history of the Americas.

An Ancient Civilization in Peru

Near the end of the 20th century, not far from Lima, Peru, a team of American and Peruvian archeologists was investigating a ceremonial center. After years of excavation and collecting materials, they determined that this ceremonial site was actually part of a small city, the oldest known city in the Americas.

But they had heard about some mounds north of their site, which was north of Lima, that many people believed to be naturally occurring knolls of land between 20 and 50 feet high. Called the Norte Chico, the area was not known to hold valuable resources such as gold, so there had never been any development in modern times. And even though it was only 100 miles north of the capital of Peru, it was still an isolated area with little road access.

The researchers discovered that these mounds were not naturally occurring. Instead they were the remnants of not just one city but of almost 25 cities within an area about 100 miles long and 25 miles wide. This was not the only surprising bit. When they began dating their finds, researchers learned that the oldest of these cities had been established around 3500 BC, with others following later, up until 2700 BC.

What makes this find especially amazing is that what many scholars called the cradle of Western civilization, Sumeria, was also being established at this time. Located in what is now central Iraq, Sumeria had long been thought to represent the first civilization in the history of our species, the first time humans banded together in a very large group of city states.

But in Peru, a group of archeologists found evidence of a similarly sophisticated society that had sprung up at around the same time. Dating techniques did suggest that the Sumerians had been first, but further study showed another discovery. The people of Norte Chico not only had these cities (which individually were smaller than the ones in Sumeria but on the whole covered a larger area), but they were also populated with people who were willing to spend their days creating public monuments. And this kind of activity can occur only when there are leaders (or a system of leadership) that can create the conditions needed for people to do so.

According to Jonathan Haas, one of the archeologists who discovered the sites in Norte Chico:

> *It's one of only two places on earth* [Sumeria being the other]—*three, if you count Mesoamerica—where government was an invention. Everywhere else it was inherited or borrowed. People were born into societies with governments or saw their neighbors' governments and copied the idea. Here, people came up with it themselves.*

Learning from the Natives

We now know that the idea of government wasn't a new idea in the Americas when the Iroquois Confederacy was formed. It was already well established. So, despite the claims by many historians (and what people in North America were taught), Natives in the Americas prior to Columbus were not savages, nor were they primitive tribes of hunters and gatherers leading lives of basic subsistence. Rather, they were sophisticated peoples whose history with government and civilization went back as far as that of Western civilization.

Having this awareness, we need not be so surprised to learn that, when the British first landed on the shores of what is now the eastern United States, the Native peoples of the land actually thought that these new people were the savages.

The Europeans were like little children, noted many Native bands after their first contacts. The newcomers could barely feed themselves, they didn't know how or where to plant crops, most couldn't hunt, they didn't know about medicines, they always settled in the wrong place and they had poor personal hygiene (most Europeans who had arrived in the Americas rarely bathed, if at all).

As well, to the Natives, European society seemed cruel and harsh. Everyone was stuck in a rigid class system that had no flexibility and seemed to make no sense; not only was it inadequate, but it also worked against their very survival in this New World. Every European also owed total fealty to a monarch or a pope (or both). They could be taxed without reason. They owned almost nothing, because anything they had—their lands, their crops, their families, their livestock—could be taken away by order of the king, and they had no choice but to obey.

Most Europeans could not choose their own spouse and, even if they did, they never married someone out of their social class. They could also be physically punished or imprisoned without any appeal. They could even be killed for seemingly minor infractions, such as disputing the word of a governor or missing church three weeks in a row.

Europeans also treated their children with much cruelty compared to Native culture. By the age of six, most of the settlers' children had to go to work in the fields or elsewhere—and put in a full day's work, just like the adults.

In contrast, Native children were free to explore the lands with their friends, to learn about their environment and how to survive in it through play. Life wasn't easy, though, because they did have to learn skills such as how to hunt, how to collect food and how to plant crops. But when compared to the rigid lives of typical European children, the lives of Native children were paradise.

Most Natives scoffed at the European contention of superiority, that—despite having developed the technology to produce firearms and metal swords—Europe was a more advanced and more sophisticated civilization.

Louis-Armand de Lom d'Arce, a French baron who between 1683 and 1694 lived in what is now Québec and frequently interacted with the Hurons, observed:

> *They brand us for Slaves, and call us miserable Souls,*
> *whose Life is not worth having, alledging,* [sic]

> *That we degrade ourselves in subjecting our selves to one Man who possesses the whole Power, and is bound by no law but his own Will...* [Individual Indians] *value themselves above any thing that you can imagine, and this is the reason they always give for't, That one's as much Master as another, and since Men are all made of the same Clay there should be no Distinction or Superiority among them.*

The Natives who visited Europe and then returned did talk of a fascinating society, but they were also shocked by the differences between the people, not just in social standing but also economically. They were dismayed and stunned to see people who lived lives of great plenty and "gorged to the full with things of every sort," whereas others were so hungry that they died of starvation or had to beg for food, as Michel de Montaigne noted in 1580 in his essay *On Cannibals* after talking to some Brazilian Natives who had visited France. Such a thing would never have been allowed to occur in almost any of the Native American societies.

The Mi'kmaq of Nova Scotia wondered, if Christian civilization was so wonderful, why were all these new settlers coming to the Americas to get away from it? And that is exactly what many Europeans settlers were doing. A large number of the European settlers were coming to the Americas to escape the rigid and oppressive nature of their Old World.

Dr. Donald Grinde Jr., history professor at the University of Vermont, made this observation in a 2002 interview:

> [M]*any people fled England because they were critical of English society and its structure. They came to*

America and they found societies without kings and nobility—where everyone was free. There was little or no inequality with regards to wealth. There was enough food to go around—everyone ate. These were not just observations of Native American societies. They were quite frequently criticisms of European society that these European immigrants were leveling, because they were among the reasons why they left the European nations to come to America.

Many settlements in the Americas, including the ones that, like Jamestown, succeeded, lost a good number of their residents not just to disease and starvation but to the country. Some of these settlers, when comparing life among the Natives—with enough food to eat and the freedom to do what one wanted and live the life one wanted—to the rigidity of European hierarchy and society, chose to leave their settlements and live with the Natives, even though doing so was frequently considered a crime with a punishment of death by hanging.

In addition, when a large number of colonists who had been kidnapped by the Natives and lived in their society for a period were rescued or ransomed and returned to European society, they chose to go back to the Native society that had kidnapped them in the first place.

Many European settlements attempted to convert Natives to the European way of life, but, for the most part, they were usually unsuccessful in their early attempts. In 1753, Benjamin Franklin wrote:

When an Indian Child has been brought up among us, taught our language and habituated to our Customs, yet if he goes to see his relations and makes one Indian Ramble with them there is no perswading [sic] him ever to return. When white persons of either sex have been taken prisoner young by the Indians, and lived awhile among them, tho' ransomed by their Friends, and treated with all imaginable tenderness to prevail with them to stay among the English, yet in a Short time, they become disgusted with our manner of life, and the care and pains that are necessary to support it, and take the first good Opportunity of escaping again into the Woods, from whence there is no reclaiming them.

In his book *1491: New Revelations of the Americas Before Columbus*, Charles C. Mann writes,

Influenced by their proximity to Indians—by being around living, breathing role models of human liberty—European colonists adopted their insubordinate attitudes, "which troubled the power elite of France," the historian Cornelius J. Jaenen observed...

In the most direct way, Indian liberty made indigenous villages into competitors for colonists' allegiance. Colonial societies could not become too oppressive, because their members—surrounded by examples of free life—always had the option to vote with their feet. It is likely that the first British villages in North America, thousands of miles from the House of Lords, would have lost some of the brutally graded social hierarchy that characterized European life. But it is also clear that they were infused by the democratic, informal brashness of Native American culture. That spirit alarmed and discomfited many Europeans, toff and peasant alike. But it is also clear that many others found it a deeply attractive vision of human possibility.

The American Revolution and the Constitution of the United States

These days, many highly respected historians say that the influence of the Natives, specifically the Iroquois Confederacy, altered the story about the America Revolution and the Constitution of the United States.

Many of the architects of the American Revolution—Benjamin Franklin, John Adams, Thomas Jefferson and others—connected in many ways to the Natives and the member nations of the Iroquois Confederacy. John Adams grew up in Quincy, Massachusetts, which was just one mile from the village of one of the key chiefs. Many such chiefs were frequent visitors to John Adams' house when he was a boy. He also visited the village on a regular basis.

Benjamin Franklin also had deep connections with the Natives. He negotiated many treaties with them. Through his printing business, he printed many of these treaties as well as some examples of the Great Law of Peace (discussed in an earlier chapter).

Over a period of several centuries, the influence of the Natives through the Great Law of Peace grew—their freedoms of liberty, control over their own property, the lack of a rigid social hierarchy, the lack of fealty to a monarchy and the pursuit of personal happiness. Eventually their beliefs became so influential that the colonists, both those who immigrated to the continent themselves and those who were born in the Americas, realized that something must change. They could no longer be subject to a king who lived so far away yet tried to control so much of their lives and taxed their goods. This realization played a key role in the growing discontent among the English colonists during the mid-to-latter part of the 16th century, just prior to the American Revolution.

"So vivid were these examples of democratic self-government that some historians and activists have argued that the Great Law of Peace directly inspired the American Constitution," Charles C. Mann wrote in the *New York Times* in 2005.

> *The framers of the Constitution...were pervaded by Indian images of liberty.*
>
> *For two centuries after Plymouth Rock, the border between Natives and newcomers was porous, almost nonexistent.... Europeans and Indians mingled, the historian Gary Nash has written, as "trading partners, military allies, and marital consorts..."*
>
> *"Every man is free," a frontiersman, Robert Rogers, told a disbelieving British audience, referring to Indian villages. In these places, he said, no person, white or Indian, sachem or slave, has any right to deprive anyone else of his freedom. The Iroquois, Cadwallader Colden declared in 1749, held "such absolute notions of liberty that they allow of no kind of superiority of one over another, and banish all servitude from their territories."*

Many of Benjamin Franklin's ideas about life, liberty and the pursuit of happiness came from his regular contact with the Iroquois and their Great Law of Peace.

Although some experts deny this influence on the new colony, and others say it wasn't as significant as suggested, there are other historians who insist that the Natives in the north-eastern United States and their Great Law of Peace had truly important effects not just on the American Revolution but on the development of the American Constitution.

The scholars in the last group point to certain visual symbols as a starting point in finding evidence to support their contention. As you may recall, one of the key symbols of the Great Law of Peace and its creation was the five arrows that represented each of the nations of the Iroquois Confederacy tied together in a bundle to show that the strength of their union was stronger than each nation on its own. Now look at one of the most powerful symbols of the United States of America, the American Seal, official symbol of sovereignty to formalize and seal (or sign) international treaties and transactions. It depicts a bald eagle with an olive branch in its right talon and 13 arrows held together in its left, the arrows representing each of the 13 original colonies, tied together in a bundle to show that the strength of their union was stronger than just one. It is historical knowledge that the original number of arrows in the talon was five when artist Charles Thomson conceived the seal.

A few decades prior to the American Revolution, one of the key figures in American history, Benjamin Franklin, tried to persuade the British colonies to adopt an alliance similar to the Iroquois Confederacy. In the 1750s, the British and French were in a continual conflict over who would control North America. As part of their strategy, the British determined that an alliance with the Iroquois would change the balance of power in their favor against the French. At the time, the Five Nations were a significant force, politically and militarily, with which to be reckoned.

In their efforts, the British sent many colonial ambassadors to meet with the Iroquois in Albany, New York. Benjamin Franklin was one of those delegates, and, through his discussions with the Iroquois, along with his previous knowledge of treaties as a result of his printing service, he became very well versed in the Great Law of Peace.

In June 1754, he authored the Albany Plan of Union:

It is proposed that humble application be made for an act of Parliament of Great Britain, by virtue of which one general government may be formed in

America, including all the said colonies, within and under which government each colony may retain its present constitution.

Later that same year, Franklin wrote that he hoped that,

...the colonies would learn to consider themselves as not belonging to a different community with different interests, but to one community with one interest, which I imagine would contribute to strengthen the whole, and greatly lessen the danger of future separations.

Today, this form of government is known as federalism, and it is a common form of government throughout the world, especially in the West and industrialized nations. But back then, it was a radical new idea to the Europeans, revolutionary in many senses.

Almost all European nations governed their citizens and colonies from the top down, with the power of the nation residing in the monarch, the church or some governor or military leader who derived his power from the monarch or the church. The idea of sharing power as equals had never truly been seen in Western European culture.

But, to the Iroquois, this type of federalism was neither new nor revolutionary; it had been the model and the foundation of their government for more than 500 years. Based on the historical evidence, it's relatively easy to see where Franklin got his revolutionary ideas.

All the delegates attending the Albany conference approved of Franklin's Albany Plan of Union, but the governors of American colonies and the powers back in Britain rejected the idea. Even so, the Albany Plan of Union is considered to be a key stepping-stone to the American Revolution and the creation of the Constitution of the United States of America.

At the first Constitutional Convention after the success of the colonists in the American Revolution, John Rutledge, a delegate from South Carolina and one of the founding fathers, opened the proceedings of a committee by reading a quote attributed to an Iroquois chief from 1520: "We, the people, to form a union, to establish peace, equity and order."

Compare this to the first line of the American Constitution:

We the People, of the United States, in Order to form a more perfect Union, establish Justice, ensure domestic Tranquility, provide for the common defense, promote the general Welfare, and secure the Blessings of Liberty to ourselves and our Posterity, do ordain and establish this Constitution for the United States of America.

Rutledge further quoted many parts of the Great Law of Peace throughout the Constitutional Convention.

Also, one of the big concerns of the founding fathers of the United States prior to the development of the Constitution was how to govern such an expansive land filled with a large variety of people—not just British but also other Europeans, such as Germans, French, Poles and Dutch, and including Catholics, Puritans, Quakers and Protestants of all stripes—and to do so fairly and with justice for all.

First page of the Constitution of the United States. It is believed that many of the key elements of the Constitution came from the Great Law of Peace.

During the Constitutional Convention, John Adams noted that the best example that he had seen to govern in such a situation was the Iroquois Confederacy, which featured a separation of powers that granted the whole alliance responsibility over certain areas, such as defense, while giving each of the Five Nations power over their own local affairs. The American Constitution in turn does an admirable job of not just separating power into three branches of federal government but also separating powers between the federation and the individual states. Adams, in his book *A Defense of the Constitution of the United States of America*, discussed the "fifty families of the Iroquois" as a model for the Americans to follow.

As John Rutledge also observed during the Constitutional Convention, "The only condition on earth to be compared with ours is that of the Indians, where they still have less law than we."

According to Professor Donald Grinde in 2002, the Great Law of Peace and other Native societies also influenced one of the greatest sections of the American Constitution, the separation between the church and state:

> *If you put the church in the government, then you get into the problem that the church vests power into the leaders. In Native American societies, religion is not a part of politics—at least, it doesn't vest power in individuals. Power is breathed into leaders by the people, and those leaders then exist on that support. When that support no longer exists, then their power ceases to exist.*

During the Continental Congress of 1775, Iroquois leaders were invited to Independence Hall in 1775 to observe the proceedings. According to some commentators, they were given positions of honor, indicated by their sleeping quarters in the hall, suggesting that the Iroquois people were respected and that they therefore could have held influence over the thought process of the framers of the emerging American nation.

Felix Cohen, in a 1952 article in *The American Scholar*, asserted:

> *It is out of a rich Indian democratic tradition that the distinctive political ideals of American life emerged. Universal suffrage for women as well as men, the pattern of states within a state that we call federalism, the habit of treating chiefs as servants of the people instead of their masters, the insistence that the community must respect the diversity of men and the diversity of their dreams—all these things were part of the American way of life before Columbus landed.*

Cohen wasn't the only one with that opinion. In his book *The Patriot Chiefs*, first published in 1961, Alvin Josephy said:

> *So unique a Native organization, resting on high-minded principles of republicanism and democracy, eventually quickened the interest of many colonial leaders, including Benjamin Franklin.... Through-out the eighteenth century, the republican and dem-ocratic principles that lay at the heart of the Five Nations' system of self-government had been included among the studies of philosophers of Europe and America who were seeking a more just and humane way for men to be governed.*

(As quoted by Bruce Johansen in his 1998 book, *Debating Democracy: Native American Legacy of Freedom*.)

When one looks at the actual history of the Native peoples of North America and learns about significant political developments such as the Iroquois Confederacy and the Great Law of Peace, one cannot dismiss the influence Native Americans have had on the United States and its creation.

To quote Bruce Johansen, professor of Communication and Native American Studies at the University of Nebraska at Omaha, in *Debating Democracy: Native American Legacy of Freedom*, "If concepts of freedom and democracy are so purely Western in origin, why did they blossom after Europeans discovered the New World and its societies?"

Without the influence of the Natives on its founding, either socially and politically, one of the great nations in the history of the world would not have come into being, at least not as we know it today.

In 1987, the U.S. Senate passed Concurrent Resolution 76, with a worthy intention: "To acknowledge the contribution of the Iroquois Confederacy of Nations to the development of the U.S. Constitution."

But there was one area in the writing of the American Constitution that Native influence was not felt.

Chapter Fifteen

Equal Rights

Female Power in the Five Nations

In the history of the Great Law of Peace, the first person to accept and promote Deganawidah's vision was a woman who owned a house on a main route between the nations and fed the many hunters and others who traveled along that path. She was simply an innkeeper who provided shelter to travelers. And by doing so, she made connections with many people throughout the Five Nations and thus probably held a place of influence and power. In recognizing her as the first woman to accept the Great Law, Deganawidah proclaimed her "Jikohnsaseh, Peace Queen, Mother of Nations."

Jikohnsaseh also probably saw how the constant fighting between the nations not only negatively affected her community but also the community of others. No doubt she saw the value in a life of peace compared to living under the constant threat of violence.

"Savagery to 'Civilization'" (drawn by Joseph Keppler). "The Indian women: 'We whom you pity as drudges reached centuries ago the goal that you are now nearing,'" which meant that Native women had more rights under the Great Law of Peace.

As was described in the chapter about the Great Law of Peace, Deganawidah the Peacemaker recognized that women have a different perspective of life and human affairs than men do. Because of their role in the family, he observed, they are able to see the futility of unnecessary warfare and the resulting grief. For this reason, he declared that both spiritual and political power be invested in women called "Clan Mothers," who would lead the people and have complete control over the men who would be chiefs.

Among the Five Nations, women had not only political power but also the right to possess their own property, including croplands and animals. Without needing to get the okay from any male, they could independently decide to buy, sell or trade such items. So great was the tradition of respect for women in this society that when a man married, he moved into his wife's family home, rather than the reverse. An abusive or poorly behaved husband could be sent packing by the women of the clan, which meant that he had to leave everything but his clothes behind for the support of his children. In every regard, the power of the Five Nations women stood in marked contrast to the dependent status of the colonial women.

An example of this power comes from a story told by Elizabeth Cady Stanton, one of the great leaders of the women's movement who fought for universal suffrage in the U.S. As Dr. Donald Grinde Jr. recounted:

> *Elizabeth Cady Stanton describes how, as a young girl on an Iroquois reservation—she was twelve or thirteen—she saw a man come up, and the mother of her Indian playmate went outside and talked to this man for a half hour or more. Then he handed her some money, they went to the barn and took a horse out, and he rode off on the horse.*

> [Elizabeth] *asked the mother what had happened, and the woman said, "Well, I sold the man one of my horses. We negotiated the price, and then he gave me the money, and then he left with the horse."*

> *Elizabeth...said, "What will your husband say when he gets home?"*

> *The woman said, "Well, it was my horse, and I can do with it as I please."*

Founding a Movement

For a female member of the Iroquois Confederacy, being able to conduct business on her own was a relatively commonplace occurrence. But for Stanton and other great leaders of the early women's movement in the United States—such as Lucretia Coffin Mott and Susan B. Anthony—life was very different.

Even though the American constitution was deemed a milestone in the history of democracy, nothing had changed for women. The roles and rights of European women in postrevolutionary America were no different than in pre-revolutionary America. They had no right to vote and no right to property, for example; indeed, white men still enjoyed many more freedoms than white women.

Unlike their Native counterparts, who gave all people of the nations the right to vote and the right to their property and personal liberties, the architects of the United States did not reach so far.

Under U.S. laws at the time, a woman had no rights to property, no rights to any earnings if she worked and no rights to any inheritance. Everything belonged to her husband or her father. A woman didn't even have any rights to her children, because her husband could assign the guardianship of his children whenever he wanted and to whomever he chose.

If a woman had a husband who was a philanderer and had one or many mistresses—even children by other women—there was nothing she could do. Even if her husband was a man of the cloth who had committed adultery, she could not divorce him.

If a woman of European descent was married to an abusive husband, there was nothing she could do. She was, in effect, his property. And if she tried to flee her home because of abuse, and even if her spouse had threatened to kill her, she would be hunted down by the police (or bounty hunters) the same way they would hunt down an escaped slave. If caught, she would be taken back to her husband despite any proof she might have of his abuse.

Testifying as to how it was among the people of the Great Law of Peace, on the other hand, Reverend Ashur Wright wrote of the Seneca in 1873:

> *As to their family system, when occupying the old long-houses, it is probable that some one clan predominated, the women taking in husbands, however, from the other clans; and sometimes, for a novelty, some of their sons bringing in their young wives until they felt brave enough to leave their mothers. Usually, the female portion ruled the house, and were doubtless clannish enough about it. The stores were in common; but woe to the luckless husband or lover who was too shiftless to do his share of the providing. No matter how many children or whatever goods he might have in the house, he might at any time be ordered to pick up his blanket and budge; and after such orders it would not be healthful for him to attempt to disobey...*

Elizabeth Cady Stanton apparently drew from his work when addressing the first convention of the National Council of Women convention in 1891.

As well, Iroquois women could not only work in the fields harvesting the Three Sisters—corn, beans and squash—along with any other crops, but they also could own the farms and do whatever they deemed fit with their harvest. During an interview in 2002, Dr. Donald Grinde Jr. observed, "The power of the Iroquois women was based in economics, since they controlled the fields and the agricultural production." He credited his friend Sally Roesch Wagner, author of *Sisters in Spirit: Haudenosaunee (Iroquois) Influence on Early American Feminists*, for her work in this field. Roesch was one of the first women to receive a doctorate in the United States for work in women's studies and a founder of one of the U.S.'s first women's studies programs, at California State University, Sacramento. "Their power flowed from that, and that is an important part of how the Iroquois defined democracy: in order to be equal, one had to have a stake in society," Grinde continued.

Some observers claimed that women of European descent were treated better when they visited Native communities near their own homes than in white communities, because rape, for example, was an extremely rare crime in Native villages. In a story in a New York City newspaper, Reverend M.F. Trippe, a longtime missionary on the Seneca reservations, was quoted as saying,

> [Native men] *have a sincere respect for women—their own women as well as those of the whites. I have seen young white women going unprotected about parts of the reservations in search of botanical specimens best found there and Indian men helping them. Where else in the land can a girl be safe from insult from rude men whom she does not know?*

It's not surprising, according to many commentators, that the early feminist movements in the United States began in central New York. The three major historical figures behind this movement, Elizabeth Cady Stanton, Lucretia Coffin Mott and Susan B. Anthony, all grew up and lived most of their lives in this area, which was directly in the heart of the Haudenosaunee.

Like their forefathers, the founders of the United States of America, these three women lived in and around and interacted with other women who had much freer lives than they did. Almost every day of their lives, they saw women who had much more economic, social and political freedom; freedom that they could only dream about.

All three were strident abolitionists, strong supporters of anti-slavery measures and founders of various anti-slavery societies. Although these three women all had dreams and ideas of what women's lives could be about, it was Lucretia Mott who started everything moving. Mott and Stanton first met at the 1840 World Anti-Slavery Convention in London, England. By this time, Mott, who was 20 years older than Stanton, was a well-respected speaker against slavery. She had been speaking throughout the United States and had had an audience with then-President John Tyler about abolishing slavery.

Stanton was on her honeymoon in England and attended the convention as a spectator. She missed Mott's speech, but the two women met later and kept in close contact after returning to the United States.

Mott was an ordained Quaker minister and, along with her husband, was also a member of the Indian committee of the Philadelphia yearly Meeting of the Society of Friends. This group of Quakers developed a friendship with the Seneca Nation and set up a school and farm near one of their settlements in southwestern New York State. The group even helped the Seneca save some of their territory from unscrupulous land speculators.

In the summer of 1848, Mott observed the Seneca reorganizing their government structure. She watched as men and women talked about their future. She witnessed women from the nation participating as full partners in the discussion and the decision-making as the Seneca moved to a more constitutional government.

"When the Seneca adopted a constitutional form of government," wrote Sally Roesch Wagner in her 1996 essay collection, *The Untold Story of the Iroquois Influence on Early Feminists*, "they retained the tradition of full involvement of the women. Under their constitution, no treaty could be valid without the consent of three-quarters of the 'mothers of the nation.'"

Mott was stunned by her revelation regarding the Seneca. Not only was this group of women given the right to vote for or against treaties affecting their people, but they also were full, equal and active participants in the process that decided the future of their government and society. This type of participation by women did not occur in any European society at the time. In fact, even at the Anti-Slavery Convention in London where Mott and Stanton had met, most women were not allowed to participate, save for Mott, and her only as a speaker. She was not permitted to take part in any discussions or to vote on any resolutions.

Inspired by what she saw, Mott traveled to Seneca Falls to meet with her friend, Elizabeth Cady Stanton. There they organized the Seneca Falls Convention, the first-ever women's rights convention in the United States. It spanned two days and passed a number of resolutions. The first document, called the "Declaration of Sentiments," declared that all men and women are created equal. It also set out many policies that society should adopt in order to ensure the equality of women. Reaction from the rest of society was mixed.

One newspaper called it "the most shocking and unnatural event ever recorded in the history of womanity." Expressing a more supportive point of view, another said it set a "grand basis for attaining the civil, social, political, and religious rights of women."

The other resolution, which surprised the convention's organizers, was one on the issue about women's right to vote. Oddly, Mott was not in support of this resolution. Her thinking was that such a resolution was too outrageous for the society of the time to accept, and that this demand would thus bring ridicule to the entire movement. But even her opposition to the resolution did not sway the attendees of the convention. They voted to include the concept of women's suffrage (the right for women to vote) as a resolution from the convention.

The Seneca Falls Convention and the resolution for the right of women to vote is seen as a foundation event in the women's movement, not just in the United States but also in the rest of the world. All women's suffrage efforts from then on are said to have their roots in that first convention. Afterward, Stanton, Mott and others focused their fight for women's rights on the idea that women must have the right to vote.

In 1866, Stanton and Susan B. Anthony formed the American Equal Rights Association, a group developed to work toward the idea of suffrage for all Americans, be they white or black, male or female. In 1868, they achieved one of their greatest victories and their worst defeat. The Fourteenth Amendment of the U.S. Constitution was ratified, and it gave all citizens the protections of the Constitution against unjust state laws, many of which denied women and blacks the right to vote. However, the amendment defined citizens as male. So, when black men received the right to vote alongside white men, women got nothing.

It was a major setback, but the battle continued. For the next several decades, Stanton, Anthony, Mott, and those who followed them, kept pushing for women's right to vote in the United States. Many were arrested and beaten by the police; when they were put in prison, they were often treated like criminals such as murderers or rapists. When some of them went on hunger strikes to protest the conditions and the way they were treated, they were brutally force-fed.

As late as 1909, an American newspaperman wrote:

> *Does the modern American woman* [who] *is a petitioner before man, pleading for her political rights, ever stop to consider that the red woman that lived in New York state five hundred years ago had far more political rights and enjoyed a much wider liberty than the twentieth century woman of civilization?*

Finally, in 1920, almost seven decades since the Seneca Falls Convention where the American women's movement first began, the 19th Amendment was passed, giving all American citizens the right to vote.

The women depicted in this statue (Susan B. Anthony, Lucretia Mott and Elizabeth Cady Stanton) were inspired by the rights of women under the Great Law of Peace to fight for better rights for women under the U.S. Constitution.

"For 20 years I had immersed myself in the writings of early United States women's rights activists—Matilda Joslyn Gage (1826–1898), Elizabeth Cady Stanton (1815–1902), Lucretia Mott (1793–1880)—yet I could not fathom how they dared to dream their revolutionary dream," wrote Sally Roesch Wagner.

Living under the ideological hegemony of nineteenth-century United States, they had no say in government, religion, economics, or social life ("the four-fold oppression" of their lives, Gage and Stanton called it.) Whatever made them think that human harmony—based on the perfect equality of all people, with women absolute sovereigns of their lives—was an achievable goal?

Surely these white women, living under conditions of virtual slavery, did not get their vision in a vacuum. Somehow they were able to see from point A, where they stood—corseted, ornamental, legally nonpersons—to point C, the "regenerated" world Gage predicted, in which all repressive institutions would be destroyed. What was point B in their lives, the earthly alternative that drove their feminist spirit—not a utopian pipe dream but a sensible, do-able paradigm?

Then I realized I had been skimming over the source of their inspiration without noticing it. My own unconscious white supremacy had kept me from recognizing what these prototypical feminists kept insisting in their writings: They caught a glimpse of the possibility of freedom because they knew women who lived liberated lives, women who had always possessed rights beyond their wildest imagination—Iroquois women.

Unfortunately for the Iroquois and other Native Americans, during the very years in which women such as Mott, Stanton and Anthony were fighting for their right to vote, the American government enacted many policies that removed Natives from their traditional lands, forced them to live on reserves either far away from their homelands or on lands that were not considered productive and made them abandon their traditional culture and teachings. They also conducted many military actions to force those Natives who resisted or refused to move. The American Indian Wars of the mid-to-late 19th century killed millions of Native men, women and children.

Because of these policies, Natives in the United States (and there were similar policies in Canada) almost became extinct in North America. Many tribes were extinguished as a result of these policies.

Although all American citizens, including women, were allowed to vote by 1920, Native Americans were not. According to the United States government, all Native peoples living in America at the time were still not citizens. Citizenship for Natives did not occur until 1924. But, even then, Natives did not have the right to vote. Voting in the United States is controlled by each state, and it wasn't until 1948 that all Native Americans throughout the United States could vote.

Furthermore, even though American history does refer to the lives and influences of Native leaders such as Deganawidah and Ayenwatha—and makes great of Mott, Stanton and Anthony—there is generally little or no mention of the woman who played a major role as a cofounder of the Great Law of Peace that gave Iroquois women so many rights and freedoms and inspired and influenced those who fought for the rights of women in North American: Jikohnsaseh.

"Her name has been obliterated from the white record because her story was a woman's story," wrote Barbara Mann, a professor in the Department of English Literature and Language at University of Toledo, Ohio. "And nineteenth-century male ethnographers simply failed to ask women, whose story hers was, about the history of the [Iroquois] League."

But there was another Native American woman who played a role in U.S. history and was remembered.

Chapter Sixteen

Sacagawea

Expanding the Country

In 1803, the fledgling government of the United States made a deal with France. For USD$11.25 million, plus $3.75 million in debt cancellations, the United States would get France's claim to almost one million square miles of North American territory.

The Louisiana Purchase, as this deal came to be called, was one of the biggest land deals of all time. It included all or nearly all the land in the present-day states of Arkansas, Missouri, Iowa, Oklahoma, Kansas, Nebraska, North Dakota and South Dakota, as well as significant parts of Minnesota, New Mexico, Montana, Wyoming, Louisiana and Colorado. When the deal was signed on April 30, 1803—it was publicly announced on July 4, 1803—it doubled the size of the United States at the time. The area purchased encompasses more than 22 percent of present-day America.

The Louisiana Purchase was a significant event in the growth of the United States and widely considered to be one of the major steps in the western expansion of the country.

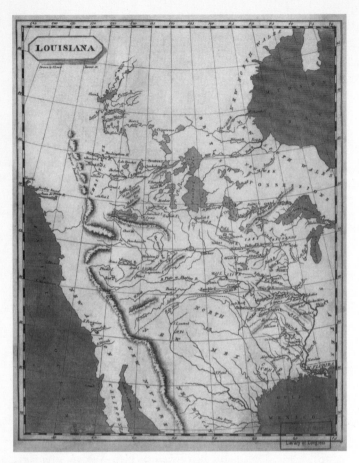

A map of the millions of square miles that the United States purchased from France in the Louisiana Purchase. The U.S. doubled in size with the $15 million purchase.

But many people claimed it was an illegal sale of land. In the 1880 Treaty of San Ildefonso, in which Spain returned its claim to this land to France, the French agreed that they would never sell the property to a third party. However, when Napoleon Bonaparte needed money for one of his many military campaigns to take over Europe, he agreed to the sale, despite the treaty and regardless of what Spain thought.

Historian Henry Adams—who was a direct descendant of two key U.S. presidents, John Quincy Adams and John Adams—remarked in his writing:

> *The sale of Louisiana to the United States was trebly invalid; if it were French property, Bonaparte could not constitutionally alienate it without the consent of the Chambers; if it were Spanish property, he could not alienate it at all; if Spain had a right of reclamation, his sale was worthless.*

Not surprisingly, most of the European-descended historians looking into the validity of the Louisiana Purchase focused solely on the European viewpoint. Not many gave any real thought to the validity of claims on the land by the aboriginal peoples who had been living there for at least the past several thousand years.

Cain Allen wrote the following for the Oregon Historical Society in 2004:

> *One of the fundamental cultural assumptions of this map* [of the Louisiana Purchase, which these words were written to accompany] *is the notion that European powers had the right to buy and sell Native lands without any involvement of Native peoples. The map has no indication of the fact that most of the land labeled 'Louisiana' was in fact a complex mosaic of Native territories, ranging from the Natchez of the Mississippi River Delta to the*

Osage of the central Plains to the Blackfeet of present-day western Montana.

From a Native perspective, France had no right to sell Native lands in 1803, nor did the United States have a right to buy them. Many Plains tribes, for example, vigorously contested American expansion into their territory. The decades of warfare between these groups and the United States is a clear indication of the fact that many Native peoples did not accept the idea that the United States had legally acquired their lands in the 1803 treaty with France, an underlying assumption of maps such as the one reproduced here.

Despite these issues, the Americans quickly set out to assert their authority over their newly acquired lands. They established a number of forts in certain areas, mostly the eastern areas near the Mississippi. They also commissioned three explorations of the territory, to determine firsthand what they had bought and how they could best exploit it.

The first expedition set out in 1804, and it is commonly deemed to be one of the most important and significant expeditions in United States history.

Lewis and Clark

Meriwether Lewis and William Clark were asked to lead this first expedition, which was conducted from 1804 to 1806. The key goal of this expedition, wrote President Thomas Jefferson, was to discover a "direct & practicable water communication across this continent, for the purposes of commerce." The men were also to map the land, especially the rivers, determine the resources on the land

and collect scientific data. They were also told to ensure that the Natives of the land understood that the United States government had sovereignty over the land and thus sovereignty over them.

Thirty-three members of the newly established Corps of Discovery set out May 14, 1804, from a staging area near Camp Dubois, now the site of Hartford, Illinois. They moved upriver along the Missouri River, and, by the time winter was nearly upon them, they had made it as far as present-day North Dakota. They built a fort for the winter, Fort Mandan.

Before winter set in, Lewis and Clark began negotiations with the local Natives, the Mandan Nation. For many centuries, the Mandan Nation had been living in expansive, permanent villages that featured large lodges, some more than 40 feet in diameter, all gathered in a large circle around a central area. This plaza was used mostly for ceremonial purposes, and at the center of the plaza was a single tree enclosed by a wooden structure. This tree was to signify one of the main figures in their mythology, the Lone Man, who was the great hero of the people who in the past had built a wooden corral that had saved a village from a major flood.

The Mandan were great hunters of the bison that populated the area around their villages. But they were also great farmers as well, and their fields of the Three Sisters (corn, squash and beans) surrounded their villages. Tradition states that the Mandan were organized into 13 clans, each clan led by a great hunter and his family. Each clan was responsible for all the people in the clan, regardless of family affiliation, gender or age.

The Mandan were mostly friendly toward outsiders, and when the Lewis and Clark expedition reached them in an area of present-day South Dakota, they allowed the explorers to build a fort. But when the expedition began to move upriver from the fort, to see how far they could get before winter made it impossible to move, one of the local clan leaders asked the expedition to build him a boat. When Lewis and Clark refused, tensions increased. The two sides prepared for battle, but both then realized that any battle would create serious casualties for everyone. Lewis and Clark were acutely aware that any battle between them and the Mandan would destroy their expedition.

Charbonneau and Sacagawea

Both groups backed off, with Lewis and Clark moving upriver and establishing a makeshift camp. They spent a very bitter winter of 1804–05 in the camp (rather than at Fort Mandan). But there they met a French Canadian fur trapper named Toussaint Charbonneau. He had been a longtime trader with the North West Trading Company, the main competitor of the Hudson's Bay Company, and had traveled extensively through the area. At the time of meeting Lewis and Clark, Charbonneau was traveling with his young, pregnant wife, Sacagawea, who was from the Shoshone Nation. In part because of Charbonneau's experience in the area, and despite his not speaking English, he was hired to be the expedition's guide as the group explored farther west.

One of the key reasons Lewis and Clark hired Charbonneau had to do with something other than his ability to guide, however. Indeed, the expedition had interviewed a large number of fur traders with similar skills and experiences to Charbonneau's. Some of them were even reported to be of better temperament than Charbonneau. But the presence of Sacagawea was the linchpin in Charbonneau's hiring. The expedition discovered that she was fluent in Native languages such as Shoshone and Hidatsa, languages that they would need as they progressed westward.

The arrangements made, the Lewis and Clark expedition again headed upriver in April, now aided by Charbonneau and his wife. Besides translation, Sacagawea also had other duties during the expedition. On February 11, 1805, she had given birth to a son. He was named Jean Baptiste Charbonneau but was quickly given the nickname "Pompy," or "Little Pomp," by the members of the expedition. Thus, while traveling with the Lewis and Clark expedition as an interpreter and helping with the day-to-day duties, Sacagawea also had to care for her newborn son. She was about 15 or 16 years old at the time.

The Lewis and Clark expedition made huge strides over the following months, making it up the Missouri to its source, over the Continental Divide and down the Snake and Columbia rivers all the way to the Pacific Coast, to where Portland, Oregon, now sits. They mapped rivers and their tributaries, discovered hundreds of plants and animals previously unknown to people of European descent, and by their presence on the land and reaching the Pacific, established legal claim (in the eyes of the French, Spanish and English) to the land for the United States of America.

They connected and established relationships with over 12 Native American nations. For the most part, these relationships were positive, and they were indeed extremely important to the success of the expedition. Many times the expedition was at the point of starvation; without the help of several of these nations, its members would have all died, and the United States expedition into the west would have failed.

Meriwether Lewis and William Clark. Their expedition, with Sacagawea as a guide and party member, opened up the American West.

But the Lewis and Clark expedition had even deeper implications for the United States. By exploring this new land—and, more importantly, returning alive from their journeys—Lewis and Clark and their maps and discoveries removed the mystery of the Louisiana Purchase and the "wilderness" that it, and the lands farther west, contained. The expedition documented the location of important resources such as lumber and furs, and it sparked commercial expansion and settlement in order to claim these resources.

The Lewis and Clark expedition is considered by historians to be a major turning point in United States history. Although further exploration and settlement didn't immediately follow upon its return, the information the expedition brought back—plus the idea that "real Americans" could travel into the wild, survive and return—inspired many others to attempt their own westward ventures. The western settlement of the United States was inspired and influenced by the results of the Lewis and Clark expedition. The two men are considered heroes of American history, and they have been honored in countless ways. Their story is taught in every single school in the United States and Canada.

Unlike with other storied events in the history of the United States, though, in the case of the Lewis and Clark expedition, the role of the Natives is not completely forgotten. In their journals, both leaders made many references to Sacagawea and how she helped them. Although there is still much argument regarding how much impact she had—many historians claim that she was their key guide into the territory, whereas others say she was only an interpreter—it is impossible to deny her importance to the success of the journey.

Here are a few examples that demonstrate her value to the venture. A few weeks after Lewis and Clark set out following their first winter, one of their boats capsized in an unnamed river. Even carrying her infant son, Sacagawea was able to rescue many important items from the boat, including all the written journals and records of the expedition so far. As a reward for her efforts, the group named the Sacagawea River in her honor.

By August 1805, the expedition was looking to travel by land over the Rocky Mountains, but they were in dire need of horses to accomplish the task. They came upon a village of Shosone Natives. After Sacagawea talked with the people of the village, she soon discovered that the chief of the tribe was actually her brother. Sacagawea herself had been separated from the tribe in her childhood, when she was kidnapped by another tribe and—following the tradition of most Native groups in North America—raised as a member of that tribe.

Monument to Sacagawea, in City Park, Portland, Oregon. With Sacagawea and her son in their company, the Lewis and Clark expedition was seen as a peaceful party by the Native groups they met.

Because of this familial bond, the Shoshone were eager to trade some horses and to offer guides to help take the group over the Rocky Mountains. During the arduous trip over the mountains, the group ran out of food and had to eat their candles in order to survive. Once they made it into easier terrain, Sacagawea found and cooked roots of the camas plant to help everyone regain their strength.

When the expedition decided to return home after wintering in Oregon, they approached the Rocky Mountains again. Sacagawea recognized that she had been in this area before when she was younger, and she directed the group toward where she said there was a gap in the mountains through which they would be able to pass. This crossing point is now known as Gibbon Pass.

A week later, Sacagawea also led the expedition through another pass that would be their final pass through the Rockies. This pass, which Lewis and Clark included on their maps, was later called Bozeman's Pass and was chosen by the Northern Pacific Railway as their way to cross the Continental Divide.

Sacagawea's effect on the Lewis and Clark expedition also came just from her presence. To many nations that Lewis and Clark encountered during their trip, the presence of a woman and her child was reassuring. In most Native traditions, women and children never traveled with war parties. Therefore, because Lewis and Clark had the mother and son in their expedition, it reaffirmed their peaceful intentions. Many villages welcomed them because of Sacagawea's presence, offered them assistance and guides and traded with them.

As Clark wrote in his journal, having Charbonneau's wife with them, "we find reconciles all the Indians, as to our friendly intentions—a woman with a party of men is a token of peace."

To honor Sacagawea's efforts in the history of the United States, in 2000 the U.S. Mint issued a dollar coin with her likeness. When the National American Woman Suffrage Association formed in the early 20th century, they adopted Sacagawea as a symbol of women's worth.

Sacagawea is probably the best-known Native American guide in North American history. But her story was not entirely unique. All the great European explorers of the North American continent—including Alexander Mackenzie, Anthony Henday, Peter Pond and Zebulon Pike—used Native guides to help them find their way to their "great discoveries." And probably most importantly, the guides helped them to survive so they could report back about their findings.

Most of these Native guides are unnamed in the history of these expeditions. However, without them, few if any of these expeditions would have succeeded.

As a final note, the Mandan Nation, who had allowed Lewis and Clark to build a fort on their traditional lands, did not fare well, despite their friendly attitudes. As more Europeans came west, the Mandan suffered from an epidemic of smallpox and whooping cough. Within 30 years of the Lewis and Clark expedition, their great nation of 13 clans that lived along the Missouri River throughout North and South Dakota was reduced to only 125 members.

In order to survive, the Mandan allied with the Arikara and Hidatsa. And as more settlers moved west, the lands held by these nations were forcibly reduced from eight million acres to only 900,000 acres. The last full-blooded Mandan died in 1971.

Chapter Seventeen

The Truth

Throughout the history of modern North America, it has been taught in our schools that the influence of the people who originally lived on this land was minimal. We were, and are still told, that this land was mostly wilderness in which lived scattered tribes of hunting and gathering primitives who left no monuments and no legacy to our modern society.

In the myths, history books and popular culture of today's mainstream North America, Native Americans are seen as savages, simple peoples looking and hoping to be either civilized noble warriors or shamans who can see into our souls and predict the future. These kinds of stereotypes are, at the very least, simplistic and annoying; at worst they are hurtful and discriminatory.

Much of the truth about Native Americans, much of what they actually accomplished, of the great discoveries they made and then passed on to the rest of the world, has been disregarded and overlooked, either through simple ignorance, misplaced superiority, personal prejudice or institutional intolerance.

Native Americans, no matter where they lived on this continent, were not simple peoples. They were sophisticated, diverse, talented, educated and civilized. Their lives were filled with accomplishment and ambition, in nations and societies as advanced as any other society in the world at the time. In many cases, the Native Americans were more evolved than contemporary civilized societies elsewhere on Earth.

When the Europeans came and "discovered" this already-discovered and settled land, the Native Americans mostly welcomed them. There were difficulties on both sides, but, for the most part, the Native Americans were helpful. In many cases, as this book has shown, the helpfulness of the Natives played a pivotal role in the establishment of a permanent European presence on this land. For the Europeans, the assistance of the Natives was a positive development that led to some of their great advances in exploration, science, art and government.

For the Native Americans, the arrival of the Europeans has not been a completely positive experience, to put it politely. Although they were mostly willing to share their ideas and accomplishments with the Europeans, much of their culture, their history and their accomplishments have been either destroyed, assimilated or just simply ignored or forgotten. Not to mention the loss of many of their traditional lands and freedoms.

But we can't allow the legacy of the first inhabitants of the Americas to be forgotten. We can't just simply push aside the accomplishments of two continents of people because we've been led to believe that the opposite is true.

The truth is, for thousands of years, Native Americans evolved and enjoyed an intriguing collection of mature, complex and civilized societies whose influence was felt not only during the time just after the arrival of Columbus but one that also continues to have profound implications for the make-up of our modern world.

This book has only touched on parts of their story. There is enough left over to write another book on this subject. Plenty enough.

Appendix

Anumber of important contributions that came from Native Americans, mostly from Central and South America, didn't fit the flow of the main part of the book, so they are given separately here.

Popcorn

Although popcorn was mentioned in the Maize chapter, this fascinating food deserves a few additional paragraphs. One of the world's most beloved snack foods, popcorn pops because—unlike many other grains—the corn seed has a hard shell and dense filling. Thus, when a kernel is heated, the pressure builds to a point where it explodes to create the food we all know and love.

Even though almost all types of corn can theoretically pop, true popcorn is made with varieties of corn with kernels that pop easier and bigger when heated. There is no definitive evidence when the first human popped corn, but ears of popcorn found in caves in Mexico were dated to be more than 5000 years old. Throughout the Americas, there have been other finds of preserved ears of popcorn, ranging from 2000 to 1000 years old. Some ears of ancient popcorn more than 1000 years old from South America were so well preserved that a few of the kernels still popped when heated.

As noted in the Maize chapter, many Native American groups, from north to south and east to west, had some form of popcorn. Frenchmen exploring the St. Lawrence around 1620 reported seeing Natives making popcorn in pottery in heated sand.

However, for most groups, making popcorn was relatively simple: they just tossed the corn onto a fire and waited for it to pop. Because the corn wasn't in a container, the popcorn would fly all over the place, creating a fun game of trying to catch the little white treats as they jumped out of the fire. Many Native American groups believed that taking popcorn to a celebratory meal brought good luck.

Although Europeans also enjoyed the fun and taste of popcorn, it didn't really become popular among the masses right away. One reason is that, before the invention of commercial poppers, popcorn was difficult to mass produce. Early street vendors who sold popcorn from their carts used wire baskets held over open fires to pop the corn. Often the popcorn was burnt or unevenly popped.

Even with the development of commercial poppers that improved the taste and consistency of the product, it wasn't until the Great Depression and the proliferation of movie theaters that popcorn became extremely popular with the general public. Because it was inexpensive to produce and could be sold cheaply, at about 5 to 10 cents per bag, many people could afford it. Movie attendance was increasing at this time so popcorn vendors began to set up their carts outside theaters, offering a great snack that was much cheaper than what the movie theaters were offering.

Many movie houses initially refused to sell popcorn inside the theater because of the mess it could create. But when they saw how much money the street vendors made, they decided to move the sales inside.

Popcorn consumption in the western world got another boost during World War II: it increased three-fold. Because of sugar rationing, candy became scarce and people turned to popcorn as a substitute snack item.

Today, popcorn is a multi-billion-dollar business, with the population of the United States alone consuming over one billion pounds of popcorn every year. Much of this popcorn is heated by microwaves, but some people prefer to stick with tradition. For instance, the Papago Natives in Arizona still make popcorn the same way their ancestors did—cooked over a fire in large clay bowls, some up to eight feet in diameter.

Chocolate

Now one of the most popular and beloved food items in the world, chocolate was unheard of outside of the Americas until the 16th century. Chocolate comes from the fermented, roasted and ground seeds (cocoa beans) of the cacao tree (*Theobroma cacao*). The beans were first harvested from wild trees in the rainforest where they grew. For more than 3000 years, Natives in the Mesoamerican area have been cultivating this tree for its beans. The ancestors of the Maya, the Olmecs, are considered one of the first peoples to have removed the trees from the forest and to grow them as an agricultural crop.

These people and their descendents began to grow cacao trees in their backyards. When the beans were ready for harvest, they were picked and then roasted and ground into a paste. This paste was mixed with water, peppers, cornmeal and other ingredients to make a drink that was bitter and frothy.

For most of chocolate's history with humanity, this was the primary way it was consumed. In Maya and Aztec society, drinking chocolate mixed with spices was an important part of life. It was a stimulant, an aphrodisiac, a drink before a battle or during a celebration. When the Aztecs took over much of Mesoamerica in the 1400s, many conquered people paid cacao beans to their new leaders as a form of tribute.

Christopher Columbus is credited with being the first European to bring cacao beans to Europe. But it wasn't until the Spanish completely conquered the Aztec Empire that cacao beans and the chocolate drink made from them became popular in Europe.

Nobles and other members of Spanish high society were the main consumers of chocolate during its early days in Europe, mostly because they were the only ones who could afford it. In a twist on the original formula, the Europeans began to flavor their chocolate drink with sugar and milk instead of peppers. They also added another spice from the Americas, vanilla.

Chocolate spread throughout Europe and became so popular that the Spanish created large plantations in the New World to meet demand. At first, they enslaved the conquered Mesoamericans, but the ever-increasing demand for chocolate resulted in the Spanish importing slaves from Africa.

Chocolate was consumed only as a drink until 1847, when an Englishman by the name of Joseph Fry invented a way of using cocoa powder, sugar and chocolate that had been treated with an alkalizing agent ("Dutched" is the term applied to chocolate treated with this process) in order to create a paste that could be pressed into molds. Fry's new process allowed for the creation of chocolate bars.

As the Industrial Revolution took hold and spread, the mass production of chocolate bars became more prevalent, and soon the sale and consumption of chocolate became more widespread.

Chocolate is now a $50-billion-per-year business, a business that continues to grow. Even during tough economic times, such as the recession period of 2008–09, sales of chocolate have continued to increase every year.

The Tomato

The tomato may be one of the most ubiquitous foods in today's world, but, prior to Columbus's arrival in the "New World," only the residents of the Americas were aware of its existence.

Genetically descended from a small plant growing in the highlands of Peru, the tomato was first cultivated around 500 BC. Its scientific name is *Solanum lycopersicum*, and, like the potato and tobacco, it is a member of the nightshade family. Although no one knows exactly which group of people were the first to cultivate the tomato, it is believed the first domestic tomato plant produced a small, yellow fruit (yes, it is technically a fruit and not a vegetable) about the size of a cherry tomato. The civilizations of Mesoamerica—the Olmecs, the Maya and the Aztecs—were major consumers of tomatoes, using them in their everyday cooking. Many Mesoamerican recipes had tomatoes in a sauce with peppers and beans, no doubt a precursor to modern salsa.

It was the Aztecs who introduced the tomato to the Europeans. Historians are divided, though, on which European first took the tomato back home. Some of them say it was Hernán Cortés who "discovered" the tomato after he conquered the Aztec Empire, and then brought it back to Spain in 1521. Others insist that Columbus arrived home with a number of tomatoes as early as 1493.

Regardless which explorer was responsible, the Spanish were the first Europeans to distribute tomatoes to the rest of the world. The plants grew well in the Mediterranean climate, but at first they were grown only as ornamentals. According to the first written mention of tomatoes in Europe, by Italian herbalist Pietro Mattioli, tomatoes were classified as poisonous, even though it was well known that the Natives of the Americas ate this fruit. In a number of European societies, especially in France and Italy, tomatoes were seen as having mysterious qualities and were labeled as an aphrodisiac. Men would offer tomatoes to their lovers as gifts of their affections.

Despite these early notions, over the decades following its introduction, the tomato began to be used in cooking, most often crushed and then boiled into a sauce. In some countries, such as France, tomatoes were at first eaten only by royalty and the privileged upper class. In others—Italy, for example—tomatoes were consumed by everyone. The fruit became very popular in Italian cooking, especially around Naples, where it became a staple in the cuisine of the area.

Tomatoes also spread into Britain, the Middle East and parts of Asia, slowly becoming part of the cuisines of those regions.

Even so, the idea that tomatoes were poisonous still persisted. Tomatoes were introduced into the U.S. in 1710, and

Thomas Jefferson grew them while he was president. Even though people raved about tomatoes in speeches and were served tomatoes at important dinners and functions, there was still a lingering concern that tomatoes were poisonous.

Legend has it that a retired soldier and tomato farmer, Colonel Robert Gibbon Johnson, decided to put the myth to rest once and for all. On September 26, 1820, Gibbons brought a huge basket of tomatoes to the steps of the courthouse in Salem, Massachusetts. He said he would disprove the concept that tomatoes were poisonous by eating the entire basket. The stunt attracted a crowd of 2000 people, many of whom thought Colonel Gibbon was killing himself in public. It is said that the local firehouse band even played a mournful dirge as the tomatoes were consumed.

But when Colonel Gibbon did not die nor get sick from the tomatoes, public sentiment toward tomatoes changed in America. As time went by, tomatoes went on to become a sign of good luck and prosperity. People moving into a new home placed a tomato on the mantelpiece to bring prosperity as they started a new phase of their lives. In the winter months, when tomatoes were not available, a tomato-shaped ball of red fabric stuffed with sawdust or sand was used instead. Legend has it that people started using these "tomatoes" to store their pins, and that is how the tomato-styled pincushion became iconic with people who sew.

Today, the tomato is a very popular fruit, with almost 130 million tons of tomatoes grown every year. There are now some 7500 varieties, in a range of sizes and colors, with different eating and cooking qualities.

Capsicums

Capsicums are types of peppers and chilies that were native to various areas of the Americas, especially in the more tropical regions. There are numerous different kinds of capsicums, including habaneros, cayenne peppers, bell peppers, sweet peppers, paprikas and many other varieties. Some peppers are extremely spicy, but others are not. Although many species of capsicums exist, the two main ones used for food are *Capsicum annuum* and *C. frutescens*. Like the tomato, they are part of the nightshade family. The part of the capsicums we eat is technically a berry.

Capsicums were cultivated mostly in Central and South America, the earliest varieties dating back to 3000 BC. They were used in the cuisines of pre-Columbian America, with almost every meal including some type of capsicum. Chocolate drinks sprinkled with peppers were also popular beverages in Mesoamerica.

Columbus was the first European to bring peppers to Europe, calling them "Guinea Peppers." Although some peppers, such as paprikas, became popular in German and Hungarian cuisine, capsicums were mostly used for medicinal purposes for their first few centuries in Europe.

Doctors and herbalists prescribed a variety of capsicums as stimulants and to treat a large array of diseases, including rheumatism, arthritis, depression, chills, tumors, toothaches, fevers and respiratory conditions.

In Asia—especially in India, Sri Lanka, Southeast Asia and China—capsicums became popular because of the heat of their spice, and their use remains important in many of the cuisines of these areas. Capsicums may not be among the most popular foods in the world—on par with, say, potatoes, corn or tomatoes—but their use to spice up our food and the cuisines of the world is almost unparalleled.

The Sunflower

Bright and beautiful, the sunflower (*Helianthus annuus*) was first domesticated around 2600 BC, in what is now Central Mexico, though there is also evidence that the ancestors of the Hopewell tradition along the Mississippi River may have independently cultivated the plant about 2300 BC.

Many of the indigenous groups in the Americas, such as the Incas, Olmecs and Maya, used the sunflower not only for its seeds but also as a representation of their solar gods. The sunflower was known as the "Fourth Sister" in many Native American cultures, because it was planted around fields that contained corn, beans and squash.

Spanish conquistador Francisco Pizarro is said to have been the first European to bring sunflowers back to Europe, after he conquered the empire of the Incas in Peru. Some historians and archeologists have said that the Spanish suppressed the cultivation of the sunflower after conquering the civilizations in the Americas because of the plant's importance to the various religions of the indigenous people.

In Europe, the seeds of the sunflower became a food not only for people but also for livestock. The stems of this relatively tall plant can be used in paper production. But the most important use of the sunflower came from the oil found in its seeds.

Sunflower oil was considered easier to make than other European vegetable oils, such as olive oil. It has a higher smoke temperature than many other cooking fats, such as lard, butter and olive oil, so it can be used for recipes that require much higher temperatures. It is much lower in saturated fats as well, and it is being used to lower the level of trans fats in many mass-produced foods.

Sunflower oil also helps retain moisture in human skin and is therefore used in many cosmetics and creams.

Rubber

Rubber is a polymer that is naturally produced from the sap of a number of trees and plants native to the Americas, particularly the para rubber tree (*Hevea brasiliensis*). New research from the Massachusetts Institute of Technology (MIT) has shown that the Olmecs not only cultivated rubber trees as early as 1600 BC, but that they were also processing the sap.

The Olmecs, and later the Maya and the Aztecs, harvested the sap from the rubber tree and then boiled it together with the juice from morning glory vines to create a variety of different items. Among the most popular items they made were rubber balls, some as large as a beach ball, to be used in various ball sports.

The new research from MIT has shown that these Mesoamerican groups also varied the recipe of their rubber to modify its elasticity in order to use it for different purposes. For example, they made stronger and more durable rubber for their sandals and more elastic rubber for bands to attach sword and knife blades to shafts; they even created rubber adhesives for use with ornamental wear.

Although early Spanish explorers did mention seeing rubber on the soles of Native American sandals, it was the large rubber balls that attracted their attention. Europeans had ever seen such things before. They brought rubber back to Europe, where it was developed into a number of products. Natural rubber, however, was sticky, became brittle when it was cold and wasn't as elastic as the synthetic rubber we enjoy today, so the products were limited in use.

For a few more centuries, South and Central America were the only two sources of natural rubber, and that restricted the production of rubber items throughout the world. But in the 19th century, the English took seeds from the rubber tree and spread them throughout a number of their colonies, such as India, Sri Lanka, Indonesia, Malaysia and parts of Africa. Soon these areas became even larger producers of rubber.

Charles Goodyear is credited as the first person to vulcanize rubber, which is to process it chemically to improve its elasticity and reduce its stickiness, thereby increasing its usefulness for an even wider range of products. Because of Goodyear's work, rubber is now widely used throughout the world in countless household and industrial products, from boots to tires and from adhesives to pencil erasers. Rubber is one of the cornerstone products of modern society.

Although the MIT research acknowledged that Goodyear developed the vulcanization process on his own, it showed that he wasn't the first to come up with a chemical process to improve the utility of the natural sap from the rubber tree. John McCloy, a senior research scientist at Pacific Northwest National Laboratory, credited the MIT researchers for building "a compelling case that ancient Mesoamerican peoples were the first polymer scientists, exerting substantial control over the mechanical properties of rubber for various applications."

The Peanut

Originally cultivated in South American, the peanut (*Arachis hypogaea*) has spread throughout the world as a snack food item, becoming a key part of many cultural cuisines as well. The oldest peanuts found have been dated back to about 5600 BC, and the plants were probably first domesticated in Bolivia or Paraguay. Cultivation of the peanut spread through the ancient civilizations of the area and farther north into the Mesoamerican societies of the Maya and Aztecs.

When the Spanish arrived in Central America, they saw peanuts being sold on the streets of the Aztec capital of Tenochtitlan. Because peanuts were high in protein and calories and could be eaten with no preparation, they became a popular food for Spanish sailors. The Spaniards quickly spread peanuts all over the world, from Europe to China to the Philippines.

With this spread, peanuts became a large part of the cuisines of many Asian cultures. They were eaten as a snack, added directly into dishes, combined with spices and made into peanut oil.

One of the more popular uses of peanuts is, of course, peanut butter. The invention of modern peanut butter, which typically includes ingredients such as sugar, molasses and additional oil, is credited to George Washington Carver, the son of a slave, who became one of the most respected food and agricultural scientists of his time. The idea, however, was not entirely new, because, many centuries before Columbus, the Aztecs were already crushing peanuts to make a paste similar to peanut butter.

Vanilla

A popular flavoring in our modern times, vanilla was completely unheard of outside of the Americas prior to 1492. Although the date of vanilla's first cultivation is unknown, it is believed that the Totonac people of the eastern coast of Mexico were the first users of vanilla.

According to Totonac legend, the plant from which the flavoring is derived—the vanilla orchid (most commonly *Vanilla planifolia*)—was created when Princess Xanat, a Totonac goddess, fell in love with a mortal man. Although her father forbade her to marry this mortal, she and her lover fled into the forest. They were later captured, and, for their crimes, were beheaded. On the spot where the lovers' blood spilled on the ground and mingled, grew the vanilla orchid.

The Totonacs had a number of uses for vanilla, such as an incense and medicine, but the most popular was as an addition to chocolate drinks.

The Aztecs, when they conquered the Totonacs, and later the Spanish, grew quite fond of vanilla and made many attempts to grow vanilla orchids outside their native region. Although the plants grew, they never pollinated and produced the fruit from which vanilla flavor comes. It became clear that the plant depended on a particular species of *Melipona* bee—a small, stingless insect that was endemic to the area—for its pollination.

Early attempts at hand pollination proved impractical. However, in 1841, a solution to this vanilla limitation was developed. Edmond Albius, a 12-year-old slave on what is now Réunion Island, east of Madagascar, came up with a simple manual technique to self-pollinate the vanilla orchid so that it would produce fruit.

The technique remains labor intensive, but it is still the only way to ensure the pollination of the vanilla orchid outside the region of Mexico originally home to the Totonac. Even in Mexico, because of the decline of the *Melipona* bee, much of the pollination of vanilla is now done by hand.

Vanilla is used in three basic ways: whole beans, crushed or powdered beans or, most commonly, as an extract made by adding crushed beans to a mixture of ethyl alcohol and water. Even with the many other flavors of ice cream that have been developed over the years, vanilla remains the most popular choice.

Avocado

Native to the Puebla region of Mexico, the avocado (*Persea americana*) was first used by humans at least 12,000 years ago. Many of the Mesoamerican tribes and later civilizations used avocados not just as a food but also as an aphrodisiac. It was a popular fruit and a major trade item throughout Central America and as far as Ecuador and Peru. Avocados were even accepted as tribute payment by the Aztec Empire.

As with many of the useful plants native to the Americas, avocados were spread throughout the world by the Spanish.

Today, avocados are used in a wide variety of cuisines, including many vegetarian dishes. Drinks similar to milkshakes and featuring avocados are popular in Southeast Asia, India and Brazil. And one of the most popular dipping sauces in North America, guacamole, features avocados as its key ingredient.

Quinine

The world's first effective treatment for malaria, quinine, is naturally derived from the bark of a genus of shrubs and trees, *Cinchona*. Jesuit priests were the ones who brought quinine back to Europe, mostly in the form of cinchona bark.

Cinchonas grow 15 to 50 feet tall and are native to Peru and nearby areas. For centuries, the Quechua Natives of the region used the bark as a muscle relaxant and to stop people from shivering during extremely cold weather in their mountainous Andes homeland. The bark was dried, ground into a powder and then mixed it with water to produce a tonic.

Many European cities that were built near swamps, such as Rome, constantly suffered from the effects of malaria, but there was no really useful treatment. Then, in the early 1600s, Agostino Salumbrino, a Jesuit Brother in Lima, Peru, saw Peruvian Natives using cinchona bark to prevent people from shivering. Because shivering is a key symptom of malaria, he sent some bark back to Rome and suggested it could be a possible treatment for the disease.

In a stroke of good fortune, the bark turned out to be effective for malaria, despite the different biochemical processes involved in controlling shivering. It was so successful that cinchona bark became known as "Jesuit's bark" and was for a time one of the most lucrative trade goods from the Americas. Once quinine was isolated as the active ingredient in cinchona, it became an even more striking treatment for malaria. It turned out to be so effective that the use of quinine has been linked by some historians as having been instrumental to the further colonization of Africa by European nations.

Before the introduction of quinine, European explorers and settlers suffered greatly from malaria. The death toll among Europeans to the disease in Africa resulted in the continent being dubbed the "white man's graveyard." But with quinine, more and more European explorers and settlers moved into Africa, and most of the continent was colonized by European nations.

Quinine remained the key treatment for malaria until the 1940s, when synthetic treatments were developed for the U.S. war effort.

Notes on Sources

Book Sources

Brandon, William. *The Rise and Fall of North American Indians: From Prehistory Through Geronimo.* Lanham, MD: Taylor Trade Publishing, 2003.

Burns, Eric. *Smoke of the Gods: A Social History of Tobacco.* Philadelphia, PA: Temple University Press, 2006.

Canadian Atlas of Aboriginal Settlement. Regina, SK: Gabriel Dumont Institute of Native Studies and Applied Research, 1994.

Chronology of Native North American History: From Pre-Columbian Times to the Present. Detroit, MI: Gale Research, 1994.

Cocker, Mark. *Rivers of Blood, Rivers of Gold: Europe's Conquest of Indigenous Peoples.* New York, NY: Grove Press, 1998.

Coe, Michael. *Mexico: From the Olmecs to the Aztecs.* New York, NY: Thames & Hudson, 2008.

Coulter, Laurie. *Ballplayers and Bonesetters: One Hundred Ancient Aztec and Maya Jobs You May Have Adored or Abhorred.* Toronto, ON: Annick Press, 2008.

Fenton, William N. *The Great Law and the Longhouse: A Political History of the Iroquois Confederacy.* Norman, OK: University of Oklahoma Press, 1998.

Fussell, Betty Harper. *The Story of Corn.* Albuquerque, NM: University of New Mexico Press, 2004.

Gately, Iain. *Tobacco: A Cultural History of How an Exotic Plant Seduced Civilization.* New York, NY: Grove Press, 2003.

Gear, Michael, and Kathleen O'Neal Gear. Although they weren't used for factual reference, the novels in the North America's Forgotten Past Series helped to inspire the writing.

Ipellie, Alootook. *The Inuit Thought of It: Amazing Arctic Innovations.* Toronto, ON: Annick Press, 2007.

Johansen, Bruce E. *Forgotten Founders.* Boston, MA: Harvard Common Press, 1982.

——*The Native Peoples of North America: A History.* (2 vol.) Westport, CT: Praeger, 2006.

Johnson, Sylvia A. *Tomatoes, Potatoes, Corn, and Beans: How the Foods of the Americas Changed Eating Around the World.* New York City, NY: Atheneum Books for Young Readers, 1997.

Josephy, Alvin M., Jr., (ed). *America in 1492: The World of the Indian Peoples Before the Arrival of Columbus.* New York, NY: Vintage, 1993.

Kalman, Bobbie. *Famous Native North Americans.* New York, NY: Crabtree Publishing Co., 2004.

Keoke, Emory Dean, and Kay Marie Porterfield. *Encyclopedia of American Indian Contributions to the World.* New York, NY: Fact on File, 2002.

Lackenbauer, P. Whitney, R. Scott Sheffield, and Craig Leslie Mantle. *Aboriginal Peoples and Military Participation.* Winnipeg, MB: Canadian Defence Academy Press, 2007.

Landon, Rocky, and David MacDonald. *A Native American Thought of It: Amazing Inventions and Innovations.* Toronto, ON: Annick Press, 2008.

Mann, Barbara Alice. *Iroquoian Women: The Gantowisas.* New York, NY: Peter Lang, 2006.

Mann, Charles C. *1491: New Revelations of the Americas Before Columbus*. New York, NY: Knopf, 2005.

--*Before Columbus*. Cambridge, MA: Atheneum, 2009.

Marcovitz, Hal. *Sacagawea: Guide for the Lewis and Clark Expedition (Explorers of New Worlds)*. Philadelphia, PA: Chelsea House, 2001.

McNeill, William H. "How the Potato Changed the World's History." New York, NY: *Social Research: An International Quarterly*, Spring 1999.

Menzies, Gavin. *1421: The Year China Discovered America*. New York, NY: Harper Perennial, 2002.

Nerburn, Kent (ed). *The Wisdom of the Native Americans*. Novato, CA: New World Library, 1999.

Reader's Digest. Through Indian Eyes: The Untold Story of Native American Peoples. Pleasantville, NY: Reader's Digest Association, 1996.

Strickland, Rennard. *Tonto's Revenge: Reflections on American Indian Culture and Policy (Calvin P. Horn Lectures in Western History and Culture)*. Albuquerque, NM: University of New Mexico Press, 1997.

Wagner, Sally Roesch. *Sisters in Spirit: Haudenosaunee (Iroquois) Influences on Early American Feminists*. Summertown, TN: The Book Publishing Company, 2001.

Wilson, James. *The Earth Shall Weep: A History of Native America*. New York, NY: Atlantic Monthly Press, 2000.

Film/Video Sources

Lewis & Clark: The Journey of the Corps of Discovery. Directed by Ken Burns. PBS Home Video, 1997.

Not for Ourselves Alone: The Story of Elizabeth Cady Stanton & Susan B. Anthony. Directed by Ken Burns. PBS Home Video, 1999.

Reel Injun: On the Trail of the Hollywood Indian. Directed by Neil Diamond. Rezolution Pictures, Outremount, PQ, 2009.

Windtalkers. Directed by John Woo. MGM/Lion Rock Productions, 2000.

Website Sources

www.bukisa.com/articles/169111_the-agricultural-and-economic-impact-of-native-american-and-european-contact

www.corn.org

www.enformy.com/dma-b.htm (Dialogue between Western and indigenous scientists)

www.histori.ca/minutes/minute.do?id=10120 (Peacemaker)

http://history.howstuffworks.com/native-american-history/10-famous-native-americans.htm

www.humanistictexts.org/dekanawidah.htm (Extracts from the Great Law)

www.nanations.com

www.navajocodetalkers.org

www.potatogoodness.com

www.tuscaroras.com

Wayne Arthurson

Wayne Arthurson, son of a French Canadian mother and a Cree father, has been a reporter, editor, communications officer, advertising copywriter, ghostwriter, freelance writer, semi-professional clown, punk rock drummer, reality show participant and novelist. Wayne has written four history books for organizations in Western Canada, as well as many magazine and newspaper articles that have appeared in publications in Canada and the U.S., including *Saturday Night*, *Canadian Airlines Inflight*, *Smoke* magazine, *Men's Journal*, *Writer's Digest*, *Canadian Living*, *Alberta Views* and almost every *Metro* newspaper in Canada. His first novel, *Final Season*, was published in 2002 by Thistledown Press, and his second novel, *Fall From Grace*, was released in April 2011 by Forge Books.